Simple Meditations and Secret Techniques for Creating Permanent Wealth, Abundance and Prosperity

Wealth Manifestation Techniques and Meditations
for people of all tastes

Scott Rauvers

Third Printing April 2021

ISBN: 9798736946648

Read the first 3 chapters of this book for free at
www.mightyz.com/contemplate_abundance.html

Other Great Titles Published By Mightyz.Com

- New Millennium Millionaire Secrets to Fortune, Prosperity and Happiness

- Taoist QI Mind Body Healing. Secrets of Longevity

- The Official Guide to Reversing the Aging Process. Rashnya Herbs, Alchemy & Taoist Longevity Secrets

- The Vegetarian's Guide to Longevity via Gene Therapy and Raw Foods

- Avoid Root Canals. 101 Homeopathic Nutrition Remedies to Stop Tooth Cavities (*revised Jan 2021*)

- A Marketing Guide to Getting Your Idea Published using Amazon & Create Space POD

- Associative Remote Viewing Technology. Secrets of Precognition and Intuition

TABLE OF CONTENTS

Limiting Beliefs And The Glass Money Ceiling......The Illusion Of Limitation......The Placebo Effect And Healing......What Is The Glass Money Ceiling?......The Collective Belief Matrix......Why Many People Are Broke By Age 65......Smash Through The Glass Money Ceiling......Additional Limiting Belief Removal Techniques......Limiting Belief Release Technique #1

Techniques For Manifesting Using Contemplation......A Simple Effective Contemplation Exercise......Remember Who You Are......Your Role In The Expanding Universe......Additional Contemplation Techniques......Contemplation On Who You Are......Contemplating On Spirit......Contemplating On Life, Love And Beauty......Contemplating On Life, Love And Beauty......Learning To Strengthen Your Powers Of Manifestation......All Is One......The Illusion Of A Single Mind......A Quick Money Manifestation Exercise.....The Creative Conscious Mind..... A 30-Day Exercise To Increase Your Abundance

A Brief History Of Money......The Definition Of Wealth In Human Civilization......Why The Rich Are Getting Richer......Why Affluent Populations Are More Happy......The Cycles Of Life......Assets And Liabilities......Long Term Assets......Invested Assets......Value......Using Criticism As A Tool For Perfecting Your Product Or Service......Falling In Love With Your Idea Can Be Fatal To Finances......Monthly Project Evaluation

Definition   Of   Source   Energy   And   Spirit......
What Is Spirit Energy?......Strengthening Your Connection With Spirit......Utilizing The Power Of Spirit......Contemplating Spirit To Create New Inventions......Can Spirit Contain Evil?......A Technique For Connecting With Spirit......What Is Source Energy?

PREFACE

First and foremost I would like to sincerely thank the readers of the very first book I published about how to attract wealth and prosperity written 4 years ago titled: **Secrets to Creating Money Effortlessly using Lucid Dreaming**. This edition that you are now reading began as a revision to the first edition, however there was so much new groundbreaking information, there was not enough room for all the text, so a completely new volume was   written.

Since that time, not only has my knowledge about the subject grown, but many of the world's leading experts on financial abundance have shared their knowledge and information with me and I have taken great pains to include the very best of what they have shared with me in this latest publication.

The prime purpose of this book is to detail clearly in simple terms the most effective tools that create positive lasting change in one's life in order to manifest their goals and objectives with as little effort as possible and in the shortest time frame.

This latest publication is a summary of the latest belief re-structuring methods, used by the top money blockage removal professionals that have been proven to create lasting wealth with as little effort and in the least amount of time possible. The exercises in this book have been designed to create for you a comfortable and gradual re-discovery of your natural state of relief, of ease and of well being and are designed to eliminate resistance   to   wealth,   abundance   and   prosperity.

The world's top money coaches (*Carole Doré, Bob Proctor and Abraham Hicks*) all preach the same thing; that **an absence of resistance leads to allowing which draws wealth to you**, rather than you exerting effort to go after it.

Please note that this book is not intended to change your belief system, but instead to re-acquaint you with the Laws of Abundance. Promises stated in the Bible are statements of the universal law of Cause and Effect; how they apply to the innermost principles of our being. Hence, if you currently are not manifesting your desires, today's leading experts on money blocks will tell you that you have limiting beliefs. This book is designed so that anyone can learn to re-align their beliefs with the laws of abundance and prosperity. The streets and prisons are filled with people who tried to bend the laws of the universe to their will and failed miserably.

As an example, if one slips and falls, one does not curse gravity as the cause, but acknowledges that gravity is the force that caused one to slip. One may even curse themselves for doing so. The fact is it is not gravity's fault that made one fall, rather it is gravity going about its business, fulfilling its role by adhering to the law of physics. Universal law cannot be broken or bent by sheer willpower alone. It is much better to learn about the divine laws of nature and learn life's lessons before-hand rather than live in ignorance of nature's Divine laws.

True Geniuses solve problems without fear,
ignorance or distractions

HARNESSING THE POWER OF BELIEF
When you believe in something, you don't need to look up information to validate it. This is because information / downloads of data will end up pouring into your consciousness out of nowhere. The key is to clearly see the images that are streaming forth from new form of consciousness and emotionally embrace its outcome. This creates a future state of mind, of being. Next you have to work hard to make this vision a reality. At a certain point you reach a stage of knowing it will manifest and you let it go so it may manifest. At this point the mind and body energetically align with the goal or objective which causes it to manifest. You begin to experience stronger feelings of self love for yourself and everybody else and take a step back, allowing it to unfold and flow to you, rather than you having to chase after it.

When you go about your daily tasks FOR ITS OWN sake, you learn about the principle of un-foldment

You can use this information as you choose. Perhaps you want to improve an existing product, follow your intuition or gain self-confidence. Take time alone to dream and believe and you will be given all you seek.

Summary

Our brains receive raw information from beyond our 5 senses which our nervous system picks up, behaving as the superconductor of consciousness.

We learn the most about ourselves and others in uncomfortable situations because old subconscious beliefs jump in and you have free will to overcome the old program during these times. For example, ask yourself the question - "What is the greatest ideal of myself that I can be today". Immediately you feel uncomfortable. This is good because it shows change is starting to take place; uncomfortable as it may feel. Some of you reading this may use this inspirational information as an excuse from taking a leap. This is a good sign that you want to change and that this information has struck a chord in your subconscious mind.

If one wants to be given everything, one must first learn to give everything up. KNOW that there is nothing to give up because nothing is truly your own

While this edition was being written, the Dow Jones had its worst month in history (March / April 2020). Therefore I believe that the timing of this book is crucial for people who want to learn how to master their money skills.

There are many people today who become successful financially, then suddenly lose it all. This edition explores this topic in great detail, examining the sole causes and shares with the reader necessary antidotes so one may retain their fortune they worked so hard for.

Living in Hawaii affords me the unique privilege of being able to associate myself with some of the most successful people on the planet. For example, the people mentioned in this book Oprah Winfrey, Dr. Wayne Dwyer and Shakti Gawain all own homes here; not to mention the numerous sports and Hollywood celebrities which also have homes here, many of which live on the island of Maui.

It is easy for one to forget the fundamentals of building true, solid and lasting wealth when the economy is good because our lives get so busy and there are numerous distractions. As the economy starts to slow down or our bank accounts begin to dwindle, it shocks us back into reality. These times are truly blessings in disguise because it returns us back to the methods and techniques that make one truly wealthy and prosperous.

Need without willing achieves little or nothing in a man's life, which why the term necessity is the mother of all invention is so true. Everybody wants to succeed, but few are sincere about doing what it takes to succeed. Great people have cultivated a "felt need". Use this book to identify your need and use it to succeed.

Throughout this book you will also find inspirational quotes under the heading - *Wise Words of Wisdom.* These simple quotes are designed to enhance your motivation towards your goals, desires and objectives.

While knowledge is power, knowledge about thyself is self-empowerment

After reading this book, you are guaranteed to have much clearer insights into finding solutions to long sought after problems. This book is the ultimate practical guide on how to use your mind to overcome any challenge.

DEDICATION

This edition is dedicated to Deepak Chopra, Dr. Wayne Dwyer and Shakti Gawain, wise teachers showing how anyone can live the good life without sacrificing Spirituality.

KNOW that adhering to the Spiritual Path does not have to involve laborious effort taken in extreme solitude. Instead, nothing is more rewarding then discovering who you truly are on the road to financial freedom.

Simple Meditations and Secret Techniques for
Creating Permanent Wealth, Abundance and Prosperity

MY BACKGROUND AND EXPERIENCE

Aloha!!! The Hawaiian Islands are a dream destination for many people and I've had the rare privilege to live in Hawaii for over 10 years and enjoy the good life; writing where and when I please.

During early 2000, I launched a successful Hair Salon product which became a huge success on the West Coast of the United States and Hawaii. From there I developed 2 websites which sold my own personal brand of health nutrition products, as well as on E-bay and Etsy developing a large following of fans. Early 2020 saw the development of a website that predicts short term stock trades with above average accuracy. My career as an independent writer has spanned over 5 years with over 1 dozen books to my name and I write articles which I post on my websites, which are shown below -

www.mighytz.com - a website devoted to my brand name nutrition products, as well as nutrition and anti-aging articles.

www.ez3dbiz.com - this website is devoted to scientific technology and contains many scientific discoveries I have made over the years, of which the majority are in the books shown on the website.

www.in2itivetech.com - a website showcasing new technology that predicts short-term stock activity.

Any of my books can be found on the above websites, on Amazon or at your local bookstore.

The above accomplishments are not shared with you to brag or boast, but to give you a sense of my authentic background; that I write this book coming from decades of business experience, both online and in the brick and mortar world. I feel blessed to have the opportunity to share this valuable knowledge and information with the world so one may find it of extreme value to further their goals, objectives and desires and avoid future mistakes.

My joy of writing was discovered while in college at Weber State University in Utah while studying Gerontology (*the science of aging*). It was not until 20 years later that my years of business experience gave me the confidence to put what I had learned into writing. My location, combined with the latest teachings from some of the world's best mentors on financial success combined with my decades of successful business experience has created one of the rare masterpieces of wealth creation ever assembled, all in one complete and simple volume.

Everything that happens to us, happens for a reason. The very fact you were attracted to this very book matters. The reason you exist at this particular moment seeking this information proves that the universe is in synchronicity with your every desire, revealing to you right now at this very moment the very answers you seek.

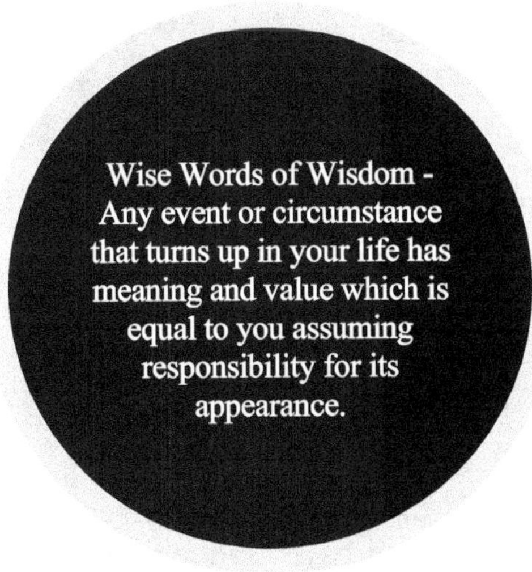

Mahalo

Scott Rauvers
Portlock, Oahu Hawaii

INTRODUCTION

There are many roads that lead to wealth, with each road being unique for each individual, so I have designed a number of unique customized exercises suited to people of all tastes. Included are tips and techniques developed by the top money mentors as well as the very best techniques for enhancing intuition which I have developed and perfected over the years. These exercises do not just generate lasting wealth, but enhance creativity, deepen one's connection to Spirit and help one connect with their Inner Wisdom. By following the customized techniques throughout this book, you will greatly shorten your effort, time and frustration required to see your goals, objectives or desires manifest into reality. Hence, what could take years to accomplish may end up only taking weeks or days. You could spend years searching for techniques and knowledge that make this possible; however it has all been conveniently put together into this simple little book. Most importantly of all, I have included all references for statements and the facts stated in this edition. You don't have to perform every single step of every exercise and technique in this edition to experience lasting results. You can modify the exercises to your liking. If you don't get satisfactory results, than revise the technique(s) until you feel you are achieving the results you want. You can do this with any of the techniques outlined in this book. What works for one person, may not work for another. These exercises only serve to show you the BASIC FUNDAMENTALS that have been proven to work over the years. The more fun you have practicing the techniques in this book, the better the results. Allow your inner child to connect with the power of the universe as you explore your yet to be discovered   potential.

Wise Words of Wisdom - It is THOUGHT that reveals the destination and your HEART that takes you there

WHY GOALS / OBJECTIVES ARE NOT MET

We trade our goals for past emotional experiences which trigger us into thinking that we don't create our reality. This causes us to settle back down into our comfort zone. We may even find people to compare our suffering to (on an unconscious level). We may think - "*I am suffering more than you today*" and use people in our lives (who are doing the same thing) to reaffirm our addiction to suffering. This is nothing more than an outdated collective subconscious program where everybody gets agreement from being "limited" in their capacity to live the truth of who they truly are. Hence, they have lost their free will to a program, either collective or individual. If do not have a specific set of goals or objectives, your mind will keep returning to the past and reliving those experiences (predictability).

70% of the time people live in high beta brainwave activity which at times is the high stress or fight or flight mentality where the brain is addressing external threats or control and manipulation of people. It is a now a scientific fact that excessive long term stress down-regulates our genes, which causes chemical changes in the body which contribute to illness and dis-ease. This is because our cells were not meant to live in stressful situations for extended periods of time.

Our environment influences our genes which can create disease. The opposite is also true, feelings of relaxation, peace and harmony can heal the body. The antidote to high stress is to open your focus. This allows your brainwaves to go from beta to alpha coherent brainwaves. Coherence creates synchronicity and it can access more resources to deal with any confronting issues that unexpectedly pop up in your day to day experience.

Gratitude has been Scientifically Proven to Strengthen the Human Immune System

At a 4-day workshop conducted by Dr. Joe Dispenza in Tacoma Washington, the cortisol and IgA levels of 120 people were measured while the participants expressed positive emotions. Cortisol is a stress hormone; higher levels are bad for the body and deplete our energy. When cortisol levels rise, IgA goes down (*which is bad*). IgA is a powerful immune system protein. IgA is much better than a flu shot or immune system booster because it's totally natural.

During the workshop the participants were asked to move into elevated emotional states of joy, love or gratitude for approximately ten minutes. This was performed three times daily. The goal of the study was to see if one was able to bring balance to their immune system just by experiencing uplifting emotions. The study discovered that the participant's cortisol levels had dropped by three standard deviations, and that their IgA levels rose on average from 52.5 to 86 just by expressing these uplifting emotions three times a day.

Reference
The Power of Gratitude. Dr. Joe Dispenza. Nov 25, 2016.

Summary
We don't need to turn to an over the counter pharmaceutical supplement or take exogenous substances to restore balance to our immune system. We have all the power we need to up-regulate our genes that govern our IgA. Hence, simply by experiencing the right emotions ten minutes a day, three times a day can restore balance to the immune system.

Stress is caused when one completely surrenders their power to the problem. Realize that problems are outside of you and should remain so. It is not what happens that determines the quality of your life, but instead **HOW YOU RESPOND** to circumstances that determines your future experiences.

Many people use excuses to re-write their ingrained habits

or to alleviate their hesitation. Examples include disease, crises, diagnosis or loss. This forces one to observe their old selves, which re-writes new unconscious programming; objectifying their conscious self. Hence, instead of waiting for crisis to you out of your comfort zone know that you have been given freewill by the Divine Creator to choose to change through pain and suffering or to experience change through inspiration and a willingness to explore. Be sincere, but willing to change positively.

Many financial experts today will tell you that your belief structure is the reason your goals are not manifesting as you would like them to be. The purpose of this text is to help one remember that nature has laws regarding abundance and prosperity. Any action that contradicts this results in one experiencing the consequences. One can avoid future frustration and discouragement by having the knowledge about how these laws and principals operate.

Keep this book and use it as a reference whenever you need to re-strengthen your connection to the universal flow from which abundance and prosperity comes from.

This edition originally began as a way to understand the Spiritual and fundamental laws of money, but after the final editing, which was a journey within itself, I discovered that the ability to generate wealth, and keep it, comes from having the courage or inner strength to recognize who we really are and to follow one's desire while being able to ignore the distractions created by the ago. This in turn allows one to align one with the angelic   qualities   of   their   inner   being.

We are all immersed in an energetic field of energy that is omnipotent, all knowing and present in all things. When one knows that something greater then one's self exists, it gives one confidence because one can tap into that greater power because it responds to our intentions. Some people call this God.

As you read this unique book, you will become re-acquainted with who you truly are, connecting with the Divine Essence that flows through you, also known as connecting with **SOURCE** energy. Hence this book turns life into an exciting journey.

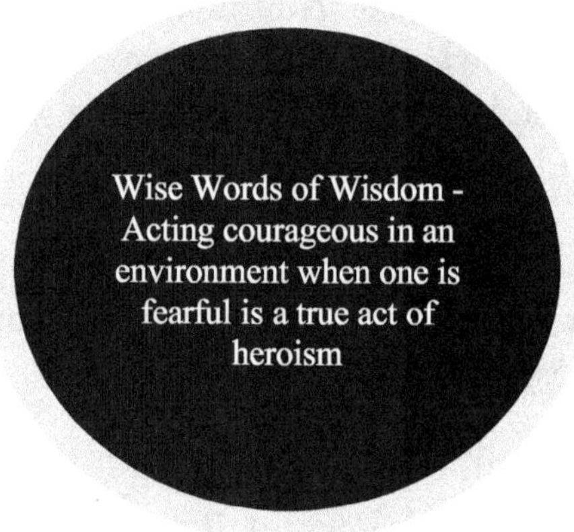

CHAPTER 1
LIMITING BELIEFS AND THE GLASS MONEY CEILING

THE ILLUSION OF LIMITATION

Did you know that if you have two fish in a fish tank and place a piece of glass between them and leave that piece of glass in the fish tank for a period of weeks, when you remove that glass, the 2 fish will still stay on their side of the tank? The same is with the mighty elephant. When young, an iron stake is dug into the ground and a chain placed around the neck. The baby elephant tries and tries to pull the stake out but it can't, and eventually gives up. The same small stake is used throughout the elephant's

You can't receive blessings if your willingness to give blessings is impeded

lifetime so by the time it performs in the circus, you know it can pull that stake out of the ground if it really wanted to, but the elephant was conditioned early on, so it does not even try anymore.

As your success gathers momentum, some people may start experiencing blockages towards further financial growth. One either gets stuck or may even begin moving backwards in regards to financial success. The solution to this is to get to the core root of the belief(s) that is causing the "*stuckage*". These blocks occur as layers or steps along the way to your financial goals and are really an opportunity for you to stop and take some time to re-examine your current existing belief structure. If the limiting belief(s) are not examined and not sincerely dealt with, one will acquire more debt, lower profit in business transactions, lawsuits and other types of money blocks will manifest if one continues on down the same rocky path.

As your momentum of success builds up speed, it is key to allow yourself to just enjoy the ride and enjoy the fun.

Just continue to adhere to the basic fundamentals of what is getting results. It is key to not over-intellectualize (*the how's and whys*) the results you are getting because your ego will start to kick in and slow your successful momentum.

THE PLACEBO EFFECT AND HEALING

The body heals through frequency, resonance, vibration, information, light and entrainment. Our DNA is the software and our brains the hardware. Our thoughts go where our consciousness is. As we allow yourself to let go and enter new fields of consciousness, the field expands and becomes more.

Every year on average there are approximately 650,000 knee surgeries for arthritis of the knee, costing on average $5,000 per surgery. A study conducted by Dr. Bruce Moseley in 1996 discovered that participants given a fake sugar pill for a knee problem recovered almost just as well compared to a group that was given a real pharmaceutical pill. This study is key, showing that the power of belief can heal. Research has also discovered that the placebo effect is effective in one third of the human population (*The placebo enigma revisited. JMS Pearce. Emeritus consultant neurologist. August 2011*).

Reference

Arthroscopic treatment of osteoarthritis of the knee: a prospective, randomized, placebo-controlled trial. Moseley JB et al. Jan 1996.

So science proves that the body can be healed by pure belief alone. Could the same be true for a "*sick*" financial condition?

Did You Know?

John Davison Rockefeller was almost three times richer than Jeff Bezos and that Vanderbilt, Carnegie and William the Conqueror's cousin were also wealthier when you measure their fortunes relative to GDP. Rockefeller's $1.5 billion was approximately 1.6% of the economy in the year 1937. If he was able to own the same percentage today, Rockefeller's fortune would be almost triple Bezos's current $117 billion.

WHAT IS THE GLASS MONEY CEILING?

Everything is constantly moving towards expansion. You are either moving forward or being left behind. Hence, you are either creating or disintegrating. As income expands and momentum flows, some people begin to feel resistance to the financial expansion. This is known as the "*glass money ceiling*". There exist numerous stories about people who set a goal to make $1 million dollars a year; reached that goal, than couldn't make any more money past that amount. Experiencing this should be viewed as a blessing because it reveals new money blocks that have appeared, without you having to exert any effort on your behalf.

Definition of Conformality - When a square peg has allowed itself to change, so it can fit into a round hole

The vast amount of glass money ceilings result from early childhood beliefs. These become limiting beliefs as we grow older. Limiting beliefs originate from deep within the subconscious mind creating "*shadow beliefs*" that shape our lives. From approximately the age of 2 until age 7 our beliefs about religion, money and relationships become firmly established. One prime example is that in school we memorize the multiplication of numbers by repetition and we learn to write letters by tracing out each letter over paper. These relationships formed by repetitive action will last the rest of our lives.

For most people the world governs their conditioning. Early conditioning by teachers or other authority figures created "*Standardized Tests*" in order to teach us CON-formality and our definition of intelligence was measured early on by our peers, family members or educators. This greatly affected our sense of self-worth. However our free will allows us to choose the type of conditioning we desire in order to create positive change.

When passion aligns itself with Spirit, miracles become commonplace

Education can only show us the basic fundamentals. If you have a dream and want to see it materialize, it takes more than textbooks to make it happen. ONLY YOU know what you need to do to make it happen and **<u>BELIEVE</u>** that you can make a good living at it. One of the hallmarks of mature self-responsibility is when one has learned to tend to their subconscious habits.

WHAT IS A HABIT?

Habits are redundant sets of automated unconscious thoughts, behaviors and emotions acquired through frequent repetition. These habits are primarily reflected by the way our body behaves. Hence our body (to some degree) is controlling our subconscious behavior. The way out of this is through meditation or similar mind techniques where you are able to change the chemistry of the body, to stop it from giving you cravings, to where the mind is in control. The body ends up surrendering and a liberation of energy takes place through constant rehearsal of instilling new habits. You have now freed yourself from the familiar emotions that have kept you in the past. Habits run like an automated software program, making up 95% of who we are by middle age and are responsible for how we deal with situations and problems. Instead, follow your desires and passion with perseverance, molding them into successful ideas and you'll meet the true genius in you; un-judged by your acquaintances. Acknowledge that your parents and early educators did what they did given the circumstances, doing the best they could at the time given the resources at their disposal.

SUMMARY

Repetition develops new habits, laying the foundation for a revised belief system.

THE COLLECTIVE BELIEF MATRIX

Habits can also become collective in the overall social matrix. War and violence for example are perpetuated by those who believe it is a necessary part of life. As the Dalai Lama once said - "*Violence and War would become extinct in 70 years or less, if at the beginning of age 5 children were taught to meditate on compassion for 60 minutes each week*".

WHY MANY PEOPLE ARE BROKE BY AGE 65

By age 25 the motivation within us peaks and by age 65, the age at which many people are broke, outdated belief systems are still running deep within many people's subconscious minds. This is why only 5% of people are truly financially independent by age 65. Know that your age or your previous background is not a limitation, but that your unlimited potential is independent of your age or background. Tending to one's subconscious habits over time overwrites outdated beliefs and lays the foundation for a new belief system to take root.

Affirmation - *Let him step to the music which he hears, however measured or far away*

Just as one needs to periodically acknowledge forgiveness in order to release bad energy, if one wants to grow financially, one must periodically let go of old outdated beliefs in order to free up valuable energy.

Vibrating atoms change their structure and resonance as you write something out, or even speak and talk out loud. Hence, when you write out your limiting beliefs on paper, in the moment, you are creating newly re-ordered patterns of structured energy that now resonate with your goals and desires.

Wise Words of Wisdom - The growth of your income is in direct proportion to your emotional maturity

SMASH THROUGH THE GLASS MONEY CEILING

Try this exercise and see if it changes your beliefs about money.
1 - First write down on paper any limiting beliefs you currently have regarding your existing financial situation. Examples include "*I am afraid of success*" or "*I am too small to grow*" etc. Anything you feel is intuitively counterproductive to your financial growth; write it all down on paper. You must write out a minimum of 20 beliefs. They exist, or else you would not be experiencing a financial *glass money ceiling*. Allow them to be revealed to the light of day. Next explore the following quotes below   after   writing   them   out   -

- *Where are your emotions in connection to these types of limitations?*

- Ask yourself "*When did these limitations first begin?*"

1 - Identify the fears around the limiting beliefs. Examples include -

- Fear of success
- Fear of guilt of having it all
- Fear of change
- Fear of change in family status
- Fear of having too much

2 - Next write out your income month by month for the past 6 months and acknowledge the monthly amount of profit you have been   making.

3 - Next state a clear intention to make $________ in the next ________ months and again write down the amount you intend to make for the next 6 months.

4 - Next align your stated objective / revised blueprint for the future with your new intention(s). For example - "*I choose to believe that my monthly profit is $_____*" or "*every day I align*

with my revised divine blueprint, doing what I love every minute of every day".

BELIEVE - that a new reality can be manifested when you are aligned with a power greater than yourself

5 - Be open to dissolving any additional financial money blocks.

Being humble enough to admit you have money blocks is a courageous step in the right direction.

6 - Next perform an Architecture Energetic Clearing Exercise, which you can find in Chapter 34.

7 - Follow through with Inspired Action

8 – Act upon any inner impulses, no matter how subtle they may appear to you that emerge during the next 30 days. They will lead you, one step at a time, to opportunities related to your objective / goals.

9 - Follow up your new beliefs with action and break down your goals into bite size pieces that are easy to implement. This results in small steps of confidence which gradually build up your momentum.

Self-discipline can alter one's change of direction in life and alter habits. Ask yourself - "*Where do I want to be 5 years from now? Do I want to be in the same situation, living the same life?*' Even just a few simple changes can alter where you will be 5 years from now. Even just making the simple decision to eat 1 apple a day causes beneficial changes that greatly improve your health.

ADDITIONAL LIMITING BELIEF REMOVAL TECHINQUES
The subconscious mind accepts what you feed it (or believe) by

taking in information and spitting it back out just like a program runs a computer. It is always in constant communication with the universe. The good news is one can re-program their subconscious mind through repetition and rehearsal.

KNOW that everything cannot be accomplished at one time, with progress being made in a series of steps along the way. Reading a book or thinking about changing your beliefs and habits is not going to cause changes overnight if it took 7 years or more to establish a habitual routine. Hence, set aside some personal quiet time to examine your limiting beliefs. New habits can be formed by being AWARE of your thoughts though due diligence and mental discipline. The time set aside more than pays for itself over the long term.

It is said that a person that has a space where they can spend time alone, free of distractions, contributes to the harmony and serenity of their environment as it helps one become re-centered. This is because time alone allows one a deeper connection to Spirit and inner contemplation. By unplugging from the world, you empower yourself by re-experiencing your true sense of purpose, your core values and your beliefs.

LIMITING BELIEF RELEASE TECHINQUE #1
Set aside some quiet time to take note of any limiting beliefs you might have and write them down on paper to reveal their motives to the light of day.

Examples of limiting beliefs include -

- *Receiving money quickly is a bad idea*

- *Get rich quick schemes are evil*

- *People who have lots of money have lots of problems*

- *There is never enough to go around*

- *I am not worthy*

- *I am not enough*

- *I am too old*

- *There is never enough money*

- *I can't afford that*

- *There is never enough time*

- *I can't make money doing what I love*

- *People think making money is a hard burden and a great responsibility*

- *More money means more bills*

- *More money means more possessions which I fear loosing*

As you write each one down on paper, ask yourself the following questions -

"Does the disappearance of this belief register in my body as a healthy, positive or happy feeling?"

or

"Do my newly revised beliefs feel empowering and liberating or do they feel sluggish and restricted?"

If so, than those feelings alone should be more than enough to confirm that it is reason enough to make a promise to eliminate that habit(s) from your subconscious. If you catch yourself re-playing these old outdated beliefs, you can simply say to yourself - *"I choose a new belief system that is aligned with my new lifestyle"* or *"I now COMMAND MY SUBCONSCIOUS*

MIND TO _________ "

Interesting Fact - Established beliefs can be so powerful that they can make even the least educated person very wealthy

KNOW that old beliefs can be replaced with new beliefs that support your ideal life simply with AWARENESS and UNDERSTANDING. KNOW that as a grown adult, that you no longer need to believe in old outdated child-hood beliefs. Habits that were programmed into you by people now long dead and gone no longer serve your higher purpose.

HOW DO I KNOW IF I HAVE REMOVED THE GLASS MONEY CEILING?

Life will start revealing things to you that you had never noticed before. For example, you may find yourself noticing small change on the ground that you did not notice before or feelings arising as subtle impulses that will lead you towards your desires. You might feel drawn to be at a specific place at a specific time, whereupon you end up meeting the right people or come across the right opportunity.

**If one fails while shooting for the stars, one never
has to worry about associating with those
poor timid souls who experience
neither victory nor defeat**

Allow belief to compound the effectiveness of all you do

An Expert is someone who has mastered something
so well, they have lost their fear of the topic

CHAPTER 2

TECHNIQUES FOR MANIFESTING USING CONTEMPLATION

The effects of outward conditions that cause us to experience chaos or struggle are only effects themselves, and not the sole cause. Learning to dismiss the emotional effects of outward circumstances can be learned by ceasing to take them into our calculations. Self-contemplation is but one of the many antidotes for this because as one learns the art of contemplation, one begins co-creating with Spirit. Now one realizes they have the power to materialize new circumstances that are now within their control. This process takes place because the expression of the flow of Spirit manifests itself as it flows through us.

I first learned about the creative power of contemplation when watching the movie The Law of Attraction and also read about it in Dr. Wayne Dwyer's Book titled: **No More Excuses**. It has been my experience that when contemplating regularly on Spirit, that it greatly shortens the amount of time it takes for a goal or desire to manifest. This I believe is because contemplating on Spirit charges the energy within one's surroundings, manifesting a type of "*Spiritual Battery*" if you will. I have also discovered that when contemplating upon Spirit while out in nature such as in the forest, birds become attracted to the environment. This is a great tip if you are a bird watcher or want to take good nature photographs!

Because science utilizes the observation of nature in order to understand its workings and create change in the world, contemplation may also be of great interest to inventors or scientists wanting to better understand nature's secrets; allowing them to create or improve existing inventions. The law of floatation of iron ships wasn't discovered by contemplating the sinking of things. Instead it was discovered by contemplating the floating of THINGS, and then asking intelligent questions why they did so.

Careful OBSERVATION is the method by which scientific advances are made. One first observes how a certain law works as it exists spontaneously in nature. Next one carefully considers what principle this spontaneous working indicates. And finally, one deduces how the same principle would act under specially selected conditions; not spontaneously present in nature. This allows one to artificially re-create the conditions which can then be patented, mass produced etc.

Self Contemplation enhances one's ability to experience self-recognition; with Spirit BENEFITING from the process. It allows one to see TRUTH. When one learns to RECOGNIZE that SPIRIT IS TRUTH, it's very CONTEMPLATION can set one free. The truth being that the movement of Spirit precedes creation as it springs forth into material form. When one has learned to perceive the relationship between oneself and Infinite Spirit, one discovers that one has free will to chose between being a slave or being free.

SUMMARY

Contemplation allows one's reflection upon an idea to FORM ITSELF more rapidly into material form. Just being alive is proof that Spirit's contemplation on life gave rise to your being born into this world.

Being a scientist, of which many are atheists, I made many of my scientific discoveries from directly observing nature, which I published in my books over the years. However after a period of time I reasoned that if these discoveries are coming from observing how nature behaves, then some unseen force must be responsible for the very act of giving life to nature. Could this force be Spirit or a type of Divine Energy that creates order?

Earth and its life are abundant and perfect in every which way and always will be. No human involvement is necessary to sustain the life in the Amazon forest or any region on life that harbors abundant life, especially the oceans. The abundance in the oceans is so widespread, record numbers of fish are fished out of the ocean every minute of every day. I reasoned that if the Divine is using us as a conduit for it to express itself, grow and learn more about the act of creation itself, that this force we call God is guiding us as we contemplate upon the Divine so that we may evolve. Hence, the very process of life itself is a direct result of wanting to experience more learning and aliveness.

A SIMPLE EFFECTIVE CONTEMPLATION EXERCISE

The secret to contemplation is to GRADUALLY let the energy build up without effort (*with ease*). If your mind becomes distracted while contemplating, than ignore the distractions and gradually allow your thoughts to return to contemplating what it is you wish to contemplate upon. Over time you will feel changes in your external environment. This is because contemplation causes changes in your environment by continued practice. As one learns to master the art of contemplation, one becomes devoted to guarding, guiding, providing for and illuminating the world as one understands the creative workings of Spirit; allowing it to become a perfectly natural process in their lives.

If you like you can place a picture of what you want to contemplate on in front of you before you begin. It could be a tree or a picture of something you want manifested. Just be sure to give your eyes something to focus on. Contemplating purely on Spirit alone is a great way to begin to learn the art of contemplation. The following is a simple exercise -

1 - Relax your body and mind. A great technique to relax quickly is to repeat to yourself a number of times - "*I'm not a body. I live in a body*". Next tell your body to relax and it will.

2 - Close your eyes and first think about what it is you wish to contemplate upon.

3 - Next focus on the meaning behind what you are contemplating.

4 - Next open your eyes and while keeping your eyes open, focus on a single point or the picture of what you are contemplating on. As you do so you may notice your mind becomes more focused and colors change in your environment or you may become more naturally relaxed. This is normal because your eyes and consciousness are adjusting to a new state of mind.

5 - After 5 to 10 minutes end the exercise.

Know that as you ALLOW Spirit to work behind the scenes after your contemplation sessions, keep faith that it WILL MANIFEST your desire. When you get confident enough after a few sessions, contemplate on LOVE and WISDOM and SPIRIT.

Affirmation - *I contemplate myself surrounded by the ideal conditions I wish to attract into my life*

REMEMBER WHO YOU ARE

Awareness reminds us that we are capable of becoming more. You are more than what you think you really are. You were formed of Spirit and express thoughts which are multi-dimensional. Spirit is made up of **DESIRE, BEAUTY** and **TRUTH**. The truth is KNOWING that abundance is your natural birthright. The ego is the only thing that separates us from this TRUTH because the ego cannot see itself in the moment.

To connect with who you truly are learn to be spontaneous

SUMMARY

Spirit is an independent principle that expresses its essence of creativity in each and every one of us.

YOUR ROLE IN THE EXPANDING UNIVERSE

Not only is everything constantly vibrating, everything is also expanding and growing; including our INNER BEING which is linked closely to our emotions. It is virtually impossible to see your potential because it is an expansive force. You have no idea of its greatness, because as you approach it, it expands. Hence, potential exists as an expansive energy that gives you abundant opportunities to create an unlimited supply of wealth and   abundance.

When we go within to seek wisdom and advice, the answers come from our Inner Being because it is connected with the NOW. Our inner being does not have the privilege of being able to look back like our conscious mind does. What we experience as the reality of now, is only a fleeting experience with reality looking back at us.

CONTEMPLATION ON WHO YOU ARE

Contemplating on who you are creates a clear channel to the infinite wisdom within you. UNDERSTAND that you are a person with unlimited potential, expressing multidimensional thoughts co-creating with the Divine.

Truth's power lies in its ability to spontaneously appear. Hence, it is during the spontaneous moments in our lives that we experience who we truly are.   You came to this earth plane to explore your divine gifts and talents

Wise Words of Wisdom
- – Recognition of your expanding potential affords you the opportunity to grow your wealth because potential does not know shrinkage

in order to enrich the world. Every single person on this planet is capable of creating and manifesting to their fullest potential. The only thing that disconnects us from this truth is our ego which is designed to sustain our ignorance. Hence, a false self that wants to remain separate cannot see itself in the moment. Don't force any situation that is beyond your control. Instead know circumstances are occurring under the guidance of the All-Creating   Wisdom.

Affirmation - *My mind is a centre of Divine operation. This Divine operation is always for expansion of a fuller expression.*

Our brains think between approximately 60,000 to 70,000 thoughts every 24 hours. Hence,

- 90% of those thoughts are the same thoughts as the day before.

- The same thought = same choice

- The same choice = same behavior

- The same behavior = same experience

- The same experience = same emotion

CONTEMPLATING ON SPIRIT

Contemplating on an objective reveals to you the infinite energy you hold within yourself. If you want to experiment with your powers of manifestation, first begin contemplating on Spirit. This will give you the confidence to move onto larger objectives.

CONTEMPLATING ON LIFE, LOVE and BEAUTY

By contemplating on LIFE, LOVE and BEAUTY, one becomes in-phase with the Originating Source of TRUE Spirit.

Wise Words of Wisdom Regarding Contemplation -

* Just as one cannot out-give God, one cannot ponder too deeply

Spirit's definition ("*the Power which knows itself*").

* If one wants to feel the Spirit of Life, one only need contemplate upon it.

* One cannot become conscious of their surroundings without first realizing a certain relation exists between it and oneself.

* Individuality complements Universal Spirit.

LEARNING TO STRENGTHEN YOUR POWERS OF MANIFESTATION

Because our thoughts originate from Source, the following quotes in the bible ring true - -

The Lord created man of the earth and made them according to his image
Sirach 17:1-4

For God created man to be immortal, and made him to be an image of his own eternity
Solomon 2:23

In order for anything to successfully manifest, you must first be **CLEAR** on what it is you intend to manifest. Be clear in the details and as specific as possible on what you intend to manifest. Every manifestation is in essence an expression of Divine. Spiritual Transformation Coach Shelly Sullivan (*Interview by Dr. Mishlove on the New Thinking Allowed Show*) stated that after going out into the forest for 8 months and visualizing winning the lottery, her intention came true. However she missed just one number when the lottery was drawn, so she did not receive the full lottery jackpot. This is an important lesson to learn, because if she had instead focused her intention on picking all the winning numbers, she most likely would have won the full lottery. Hence, being very specific about what you want is very important.

Thought that has produced the FORMS we see, feel and

experience, which itself is capable of thinking. Pure Thought is the only possible source from which existing creation could ever have come into existence.

The very first stage in the Creative Process is **FEELING** which comes from deep within. By changing the way you feel, it causes a ripple effect in the exterior world because the universe RESPONDS to feeling. This unveils the path to one now being guided by the universe. One need no longer force any situation that is beyond their control. Instead, know that circumstances are now occurring under the guidance of the All-Creating Wisdom.

ALL IS ONE

The great scientist Alhazen stated - "*If all images that enter our eyes converge upon a single mathematical point in space; which is indivisible, than all things that we observe from a great distance will appear as ONE; being indivisible by nature*".

In simple terms, this means that no matter where you stand in the observable universe; as you look out into the distance, your eyes always perceive distant objects as being a single object. For example, when astronauts took pictures of earth while on the moon, the earth appeared **AS ONE** single round planet. However, we do not perceive this while standing on the ground, going about our daily tasks. Hence, **ALL IS ONE**.

THE ILLUSION OF A SINGLE MIND

The thoughts that we experience are brought about by a 2 way process. While we may experience our thoughts as singular forms of energy forming sentences in our mind, the reality is that what we perceive as a single thought is really the result of 2 separate components composed as one (*our subconscious mind and or conscious waking thoughts*).

A QUICK MONEY MANIFESTATION EXERCISE

Some people have had luck performing this exercise before visiting a casino, or when they are in an environment where an opportunity to receive large sums of money is present.

1 - Release all resistance to attracting money.

2 - Recognize and acknowledge that something greater than yourself exists.

3 - Next become one with the force that you recognize as greater than yourself.

For example -

Hold some paper money in your hands and as you smell the money recite - "*I am one with a tremendous and vast amount of money*". Repeat this a minimum of 17 times. Next detach and let go, allowing the results to manifest themselves.

THE CREATIVE CONSCIOUS MIND

This is the thinking process associated with willpower, focus and discipline. It is also called the "*monkey mind*" because it constantly experiences a flow of mental chatter that is normally beyond our control. This mental chatter comes from our ego's attempt to dance to the beat of rhythms that exist outside of us. Many of these thoughts can distract you and are usually unwanted and can be destructive. Learn to have more emotion for your vision than you do for the emotional distractions that unexpectedly materialize. Where you place your attention is where you place your energy.

SUMMARY

Conscious awareness is like a glacier. The visible 10% of the iceberg above the waterline is our waking conscious mind, with the remaining 90% below the surface being our subconscious mind. Learning to merge our heart with our desire into a single form of energy generates **FEELINGS** which the universe responds to, creating change. This could be where the saying comes from – *"He never wore the same pair of socks twice"* because new socks inspire FEELINGS of wealth and prosperity.

Later on in this book I will teach you the most effective methods of how to align your heart with your desire in order to experience above average results while manifesting your desires.

> **Affirmation** - *I am more powerful today than the old programs I adopted in my early childhood*

A 30-DAY EXERCISE TO INCREASE YOUR ABUNDANCE

Twice per day – once in the morning and again in the afternoon, express gratitude, appreciation and thankfulness for all the good in your life. Do this sincerely and with clear intent.

Practice this diligently for a minimum of 1 month.

You will find that after 1 month of this simple exercise that you will have more good things show up in your life. This is because the feelings of gratitude and appreciation gradually build up as a series of waves, which eventually reaches a tipping point. At this tipping point, more good things begin entering in your life.

CHAPTER 3
A BRIEF HISTORY OF MONEY

Before paper money was introduced into society, barter was the main type of exchange for services rendered. After a period of barter, symbols on paper were used to **place value** upon the services rendered or objects received. It was when paper money became a part of national commerce that nation sates were born.

The Chinese originally issued coins made of iron which people deposited with merchants who then exchanged them for printed receipts because the iron was too heavy to carry or was vulnerable to theft. In 1666 the Swiss Stockholm bank began issuing paper money.

The largest gold coin weighs 68 pounds (30 kilos) and was made by the Austrian Mint in 2004. It is worth more than $10,000 Euros

THE DEFINITION OF WEALTH IN HUMAN CIVILIZATION

Money is a collective agreement on how much we value something in exchange for services rendered. Hence, I perform a service or sell you a product that you see as valuable and in exchange for that service or product, you agree to reward me with something I find of value. Hence, money is not a cause, but is the completion of a cycle or event. When you provide more service than what you are being paid for you will learn to RECOGNIZE there is NO LIMIT to the amount of wealth you can accumulate. The only lack is when you settle for less.

FAST FACT - Just 161,000 tons of gold have been mined throughout recorded history; enough to fill just 2 Olympic sized swimming pools and 50% of this has been extracted only within the last 50 years due to new technology. Currently the remaining gold below the ground is estimated to be approximately 50,000 tones, according to the US Geological Survey. Based on this estimate, there is approximately 20% of gold remaining in the earth to be mined. No more large scale gold deposits are forecast to be discovered in the near future

Did you know? The first ever coin minted by the United States Government was in 1787 and called the Fugio coin (*pictured*).

WHY THE RICH ARE GETTING RICHER

The only reason people seem to be getting richer today is because THERE ARE MORE PEOPLE BECOMING RICHER.

The Number of billionaires in the United States from 1987 to 2012

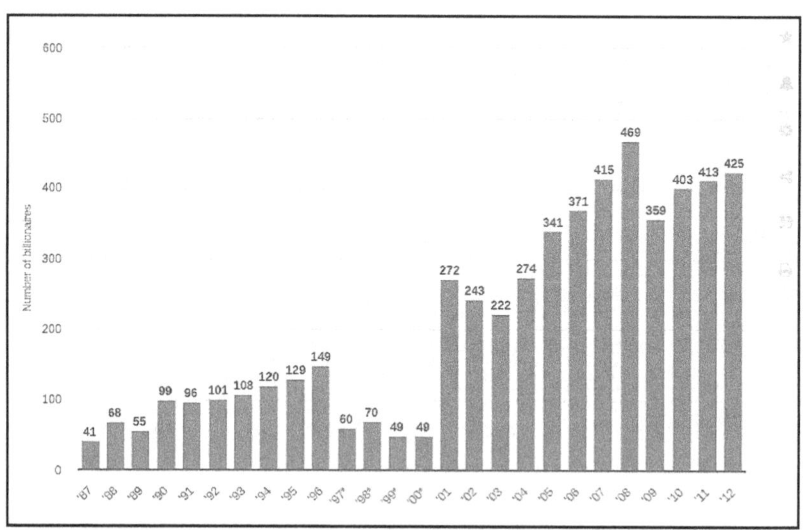

Reference

www.statista.com

WHY AFFLUENT POPULATIONS ARE MORE HAPPY

A research study that was published in 2019 by Mohsen Joshanloo and colleagues titled: *A multidimensional understanding of prosperity and well-being at country level,* examined how happy people were in every country around the world. The study looked at well-rested, friendship opportunities, enjoyment and future life satisfaction. The definition of happiness was defined as living a worthwhile, hopeful and enjoyable life that involved pleasant states of mind while developing and exercising personal and social skills.

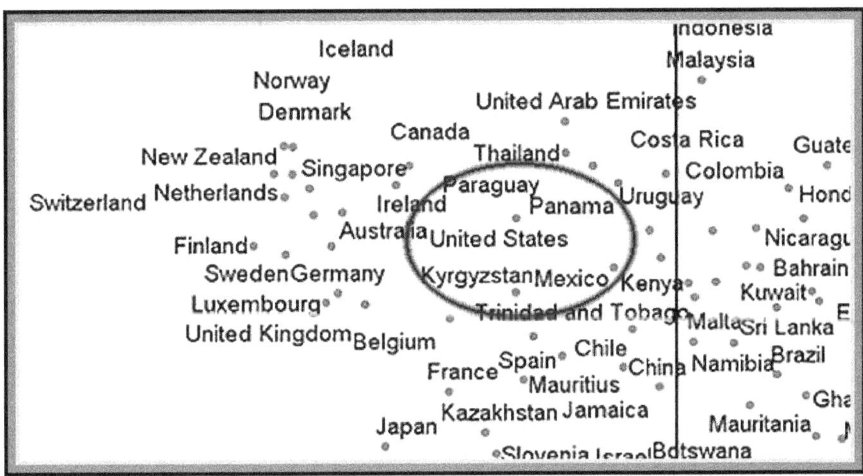

What was most interesting was that the nations that had the happiest people were also some of the most prosperous. These countries were Switzerland, Finland, Norway, New Zealand, Sweden, the Netherlands, Denmark, Canada, Germany and Australia. The United States came in around a third from the top 10. The study also found that happiness was not directly related to how satisfied one felt, with some participant's stating that satisfaction brought them happiness, but with others saying it did not.

SUMMARY

Attaining wealth is not just about money, it is about seeking an enjoyable life that is worthwhile and enjoying the opportunities of satisfaction and friendship that come with it.

Looking at abundance with anger or envy causes you to exclude yourself. Making more money does not take away from others; instead it inspires others and creates opportunities. The Rich Get Richer because they focus on what IS, WHAT THEY HAVE, rather than what isn't and have learned to not let negative circumstances stop them from going after what they truly desire. KNOW it is not what happens that determines the quality of your life, but instead **HOW YOU RESPOND** to the circumstances that determines your future experiences. The key is to discover *YOUR* purpose and allow it to full your inner cup, which in turn inspires others.

The below phrases come from quotes in the bible and are known as "*The Matthew Effect*' for short. It simply means that those who see themselves as prosperous attract more of the same. It also means by having the right state of mind (*abundance consciousness*).

Whoever has will be given more, and he will have an abundance. Whoever does not have, even what he has will be taken away from him. Matthew 25:29

I tell you, that to every one who has, more will be given; but from him who has not, even what he has will be taken away. Luke 19:26, RSV.

These quotes from the bible are similar to the lyrics in the once popular television program Flashdance. One of the lyrics is simple, yet so true. The lyric is "*bein' is believin*"

Another saying is *Feeling is Healing*.

THE CYCLES OF LIFE

The amount of money we experience in our lives, flows in and out like the tides of the ocean. Hence, disaster may unexpectedly strike after one has experienced a time of financial abundance. Periods of when the money flow contracts in our lives may be short or long depending upon the cycle. The wise person has learned to be ready for the unexpected and can wait out any storm. KNOW that when the flow of money returns, that the money will return in greater measure than before, as long as one keeps the faith, remaining vigilant to thoughts of scarcity and lack.

ASSETS AND LIABILITIES

The wealthy have learned to invest in assets. This means they have learned to have their money work for them, instead of them wasting valuable time working for it. For example, a person who owns an apartment complex that turns a monthly profit is an asset. A person who buys a house, but pays a mortgage has a liability. A person who buys a Ferrari has an asset because it increases in value over time.

The harvest is hard work, but do it without complaint, because peace of mind comes from having everything you need to live comfortably when the flow of money contracts

LONG TERM ASSETS

A person who buys a house or property that is expected to grow in value in the future has just invested in a long term asset. For example, many people in my neighborhood own homes that they don't live in, but use as vacation homes. Over time when they decide to sell their house, they will most likely get 2 or even 3 times what they originally paid for it. Hence a good long term asset will keep the pace with or even outperform inflation.

INVESTED ASSETS

These are assets that you expect to grow in value over time. A vegetable garden is an invested asset because you don't have to pay money in the future for vegetables, only the seeds, water, time and fertilizer. Over time you will reap the rewards of not having to pay for vegetables or fruits. You can also leverage your assets. For example, instead of creating a vegetable garden from scratch, grow your food using hydroponics. This means no soil is necessary, it requires less labor and reduces the amount of labor necessary to maintain it. There are many ways to leverage assets, simply use your imagination to discover more.

VALUE

The time and service we put towards something is in direct proportion to its value. For example, two people can work for the same company, with one making more money than the other. The person that earns more money has learned to bring more value to the company. Another example is that if you are a jeweler and it used to take you 6 weeks to create and set a diamond ring and new technology has become available that allows you to set the same ring in 2 days, people will see less value in your ring. Hence there are 2 ways to avoid loss of **VALUE** in this situation.

1 - Keep the manufacturing process to yourself. This also avoids the market becoming over saturated.

2 - Think of ways to create more value when you perform your service.

Citing another example, a beginning locksmith may find it takes him 15 minutes to open a lock for a client and the client is charged $100. However the experience the locksmith has gained over time allows him to open the same type of lock in just under 3 minutes, but he still charges $100. Hence, do you think a customer is more likely to feel satisfaction paying $100 for something that took only 3 minutes or something that took

15   minutes?

Perceived value, for example is when a person writes a daily blog, than takes a break for a few days or weeks. This creates a demand in the eyes of the audience, thus creating perceived value of the blogger. Hence the saying: *Absence makes the heart grow fonder.*

Find ways to create lots of value through a service that improves someone's life and give expanded service to as many people as possible. You want consistent high quality value combined with personalized service and to perform this in quantity. How can you tell how well you are doing with this? The results will appear in your monthly sales totals.

SUMMARY

Always give 100% every time to what you are being paid to do and charge your fees according to the amount of value you are offering. Find creative ways to create extra value for your service as you get better at it or sell an improved product. It is key that you learn to strike a balance between the value in the service you are providing and what you charge your customers.

USING CRITICISM AS A TOOL FOR PERFECTING YOUR PRODUCT OR SERVICE

Feedback received from critics can be a valuable tool; giving you advice that can be utilized to improve your product or service. There are times however the critics should not be taken seriously. Over time a good product or service will lessen the possibility of attacks from critics. Hence; it becomes easy to deflect the critics when you have a solid and firm belief in your product or service or what you have to offer and you have built up a 5-star business reputation.

FALLING IN LOVE WITH YOUR IDEA CAN BE FATAL TO FINANCES

If an eager entrepreneur starts a new business and it becomes popular at first, developing a momentum all on its own, and over time the business starts losing money, yet the person still wants to hang onto it, the business has now become a mind trap. This is known as falling in love with your idea. Falling in love with your idea can turn into an addiction, which is the result of not being able to define what is real.

> *To break out of an addiction one only need remind oneself that <u>the situation or habit is not truly 100% pleasurable</u> in and of itself - it is only <u>your habit</u> that <u>makes you believe</u> it is pleasurable*

Falling in love with an idea that is not working out as you expected, also is not fundamentally sound over the long term. If you are a scientist or researcher that does not mind working long hours for low pay because you are trying to perfect something and have a long term investment in it, and have the necessary resources to hold you over until your investment pays off, just know that this is not going to make you rich short term. If your original goal was to have increased profit month after month, year after year and it is not working out, just because you invested a lot of time and effort in something and it is not working out, should not be an excuse for your ego to take the steering wheel. In a situation like this, it takes courage to admit defeat. KNOW you are on the wrong path, even if you have years   invested   in   it.

If things are not working, it is okay to realize it is not meant for you and that giving up will only allow you to   see the new possibilities that exist. The trick is to know when to pull back and ask yourself "*Is this idea leading me nowhere?*"

Wise Words of Wisdom - Humility precedes honor

MONTHLY PROJECT EVALUATION
Ask yourself - "*Is this project working out the way I intended it to?*"

or

"Do I need this suffering, or is this perseverance necessary to get my plan into motion in order to develop momentum? "

or

"Is this idea not right for its time and do I need to wait for things to change or demand to begin? "

or

"Am I committed to this project for the long term to make new discoveries or to perfect something?"

or

"Do I have the necessary resources to keep me covered over the long term as I pursue my desire?"

or

"Is my ego trying to avoid self-evaluation of my progress because it likes the safe and familiar?"
or similar questions such as

Is my plan realistic? Am I missing certain components? Do I need to re-evaluable my belief structure?

It is key to **EVALUATE** your progress along the way. Allow for small changes to naturally occur, as the path to seeing a new goal fully realized is not always followed 100% to the letter.

Wise Words of Wisdom - Nothing is in reality either unpleasant or pleasant by nature; but all things become routine by repetitive habits

Change is the nature of life and its hope

CHAPTER 4
DEFINITION OF SOURCE ENERGY AND SPIRIT

While this book is not about philosophical virtues, in order to understand abundance, it is important to have a basic understanding of the forces that motivate it. In simple terms, Spirit and Source cause us to EXPERIENCE abundance and prosperity through our FEELINGS. By understanding this simple principle and how it operates gives one a much clearer picture of where motivation first begins and how to tap into it at will, especially when we feel powerless, which happens to all of us at certain times throughout our lives.

It is my belief that the Human Spirit is composed of the following:

- 60% Subconscious
- 15% Spiritual
- 25% Emotional

WHAT IS SPIRIT ENERGY?

Spirit is the energy that works in the background, much like computer software runs a computer. Because SPIRIT is always moving forward, we have no choice but to flow along with it, allowing us to make the very best use of our existing conditions in a cheerful tone. It is the nature of the Source of Spirit to manifest **INCREASE** in order that it may better express itself through us, and for us because we are always in harmony with it.

HOW DO I LISTEN FOR SPIRIT?

When you take a pause or break from your normal routine, a re-kindling of desire re-surfaces. This desire holds clues to your true purpose in life because the information is coming from spirit. Spirit speaks to us when we are most relaxed and not doing anything that is important. Its energy speaks to us in subtle whispers, an inner urging that urges one to do something or change direction or start something new.

Spirit has Intelligence and guides the workings of all of life. As we are born, throughout life we learn to reproduce Spirit as the spring of Original Life within ourselves. The life-giving tendency of Spirit utilizes the element of INDIVIDUAL PERSONALITY in all its form as the Life and Substance of the universe. Hence, when one contemplates Spirit, one begins to feel life being drawn directly from Spirit, experiencing the same thinking power that lies dormant within it. One only experiences limitations if one tries to force the action of Spirit. Eventually one learns that this occurs because we believe it to be the last resort or our egos see it as the easy way out because we do not believe in SOURCE Spirit as a FORMING power.

STRENGTHENING YOUR CONNECTION WITH SPIRIT

A simple technique to strengthen your connection to Spirit is to sincerely ask - "*How may I serve*?" Repeat this phrase over and over either out loud (in private) or in your mind if you don't feel any results at first.

UTILIZING THE POWER OF SPIRIT

When you respect the Spirit in something that you find unbearable or chaotic, the chaos calms down and you find yourself in control. For example, if you are a pilot and suddenly find your plane becoming buffeted by strong winds, making flying extremely difficult, instead of trying to fight the wind and becoming resistant to the wind, recite the phrase -

"I respect the Spirit of the wind"

or

"I respect the Spirit of nature"

or

"I respect the power of nature and beg its pardon"

Handy Hint - If you are a scientist or chemist probing the secrets of nature and prone to lab accidents, respect the spirit of the elements or chemicals you are working with and you will have far fewer lab accidents.

CONTEMPLATING SPIRIT TO CREATE NEW INVENTIONS

All scientific achievements are gained by the simple uniform method of asking questions, enquiring what is the cause and effect in any existing combination and asking why it does not act beyond certain limits. What makes this or that a success? What prevents it from going further? etc. After careful consideration of what makes it work, we see the conditions which enable it to express itself more fully. Because this method has proved itself true in respect to science, there is no reason why it should not be equally reliable in respect to Spiritual things.

As one learns that contemplation of Spirit is the true creative force, one soon learns that Spirit exists at the Quantum Level. The light that enters your eyes is made up of a series of photons that behave as waves. These waves rise and fall like waves in an ocean. At the crests of these waves, in-between each moment, exists possibilities. What the mind is most focused upon the most at the crests of these waves attracts circumstances, situations and events (*via divine spirit*) into our everyday waking experience. As you focus your attention on something long enough you can feel these waves or oscillations and the possibilities that exist between the crests of these waves. Over time this builds up a momentum all its own until a climax of energy or a tipping point is reached.

The only self-imposed limits we experience are when we are in ignorance of the inherent creativeness of Spirit which is caused by the ego seeing our body as separate from life of Spirit. Our **REALIZATION** of our relationship to Infinite Spirit is formed by our innate Spiritual attitude as it emerges from our consciousness. The whole Secret of Life exists in KNOWING that when one relies upon Spirit, that Spirit will forge a stronger connection within us.

Consciousness is the sole cause of our circumstances; as conditions cause the effect. This is why a major problem can't be fixed until there is a shift or change in consciousness. When the universe was born of thought, at the starting moment of creation no conditions existed. Hence workings of the Creative Mind upon itself could only exist as a state of consciousness. The Creative Process is not physical: its livingness consists in thought and feeling. There is something in the work of an artist which mirrors original creation. An artist creates something out of nothing; therefore he starts from simple feelings. This means the production of something beyond what has gone before; something entirely new; proceeding through an act of orderly growth. Because the Divine cannot change its inherent nature, it has to operate in the same manner as all of Life, moving forward to produce new conditions in advance of any that have gone before. This clearly illustrates the Creative Order—from states of Disorder to states of Order. However, in our day to day lives we invert this order, seeking to CREATE from conditions to states. For example, "*If I had such and such conditions in my life, they would produce the feelings which I desire*".

For most of us, we believe that we have to wait for changes on the outside to occur in order to experience changes to the inside. For example, we can't wait for our success to materialize in order to feel empowered or we can't wait for wealth to manifest in order to feel abundant or for healing to take place in order to feel whole again etc. These are outdated concepts and beliefs that require excess strain and effort. Do you have the dedication and self-discipline to teach your body emotionally what your future is going to feel like before its made manifest?

For many of us, we believe that we have to wait for changes on the outside to occur in order to experience changes on the inside. For example, we can't wait for our success to materialize in order to feel empowered or we can't wait for wealth to manifest in order to feel abundant or for healing to take place in order to feel whole again etc. These are outdated concepts and beliefs that require excess physical strain and effort. Do you have the dedication and self-discipline to teach your body emotionally what your future is going to feel like before its made manifest by constantly practicing guided imagery or rehearsing visualization?

CAN SPIRIT CONTAIN EVIL?

The root of all evil is ignorance through the denial of Spirit's power to produce good on a consistent basis. When we realize that Spirit is finding its own individualization within us, then we see that it must be both able and WILLING to constantly create for us nothing but good. Ignorance creates separation which generates feelings of lack and resistance, laying fertile ground for evil to take root.

A TECHINQUE FOR CONNECTING WITH SPIRIT

This technique works extremely well if you are an artist, because it allows one to clearly connect with their divine potential. To connect with the power of Spirit perform the following steps –

1 - Say "*I tune into and **ACKNOWEDGE** the Divine Love that exists all around me*".

2- Next Say "*My Heart is filled with the pure Divine Love that exists all around me*".

3 - Next say - "I am in a **CLEAR, OPEN, RECEPTIVE** state, filling myself ONLY with the power and the presence of the Divine and ONLY that."

4 - Next ask the question - "What is God's highest idea for me to _________________________ "

5 - Next immediately jot down any ideas or inspiration that flows into your mind.

If you are artist, immediately start painting / sketching. This method works extremely well for computer graphics or computer art. Compare your works of art to when you invoked Divine Spirit and when you did not invoke Divine Spirit and you will notice a dramatic difference in the contrast and vibrancy of your artwork.

A handy tip to help you if you are a rock climber, is before you start rock climbing repeat - "*Divine spirit paves my way*". Reciting this as you climb can greatly alleviate fear and enhance your self confidence,

WHAT IS SOURCE ENERGY?

The Divine is a manifestation of Source. This method of manifestation is known as **5th Dimensional Manifesting** (*see chapter 7*). An example of our soul experiencing Source energy is when we align ourselves with the Divine and experience a strong flow of energy flowing through us. This flow is in direct proportion to the center of yourself where the God within abides. Every now and then our soul's connection with the Divine becomes weak and we lose touch with who we truly are.

Source is pure clear energy that is completely devoid of material form or substance and is Supreme Beauty, or Wisdom. Because we exist as Spiritual beings living in a human body, we experience source FORMING our feelings and thoughts into shapes that adjust to the fullest expression of life as it flows in and through us.

By quieting one's thoughts, being mindful and experiencing awareness, we immediately connect with Source. It is from this that our inner being springs forth, consisting of **DESIRE, BEAUTY** and **TRUTH**. As our soul begins experiencing

The Law of Motion - Because source is energy in motion, when you tune into source and ask it questions, you will always receive the answer as long as you are open and willing.

source energy moving through it, it knows nothing of struggle, frustration or lack. This is because your soul is bigger than your ego's excuses. Source is bound by Universal Law, which dictates that we never need be troubled about future conditions because the All-Originating Power is always working through us and for us and produces the conditions required for the expression of **LIFE, LOVE** and **BEAUTY** of which it is. Clear and definite intention forms our thoughts and feelings into forms expressing those of SOURCE, allowing one to experience the conception of new ideals vitalized by an inner power, enabling one to bring them into complete manifestation.

The fundamentals of our universe exist as a series of independent casual relationships that are experienced as order by the rational mind and therefore can be expressed in logical mathematical equations. It is this logical relationship with the universe that enables us to "*dial into*" Source Energy at will.

The Divine Spark within each and every one of us is like a raindrop of a rainbow, with billions of tiny water droplets floating in the air with one of these droplets representing you. Understand that since you must be what you came from, just your mere experiencing the here and now makes you worthy, loveable and Godlike.

SOURCE flows through us at all times just as electricity flows through the wires to light up a light bulb. SOURCE energy cannot alter its true natural flow. Hence, its self-contemplation exists as we experience its energy flowing through us, experiencing its creative acts in and of itself. Each one of us exists as an individual reflection of what we realize God to be in relationship to ourselves. By learning to allow SOURCE to flow to and through us, we learn to trust its formative quality. One becomes like the engineer who submits to the laws of electricity, in order to apply them to some specific purpose. Hence, one becomes a distributing centre of SOURCE energy; by neither trying to lead it like a blind force, or being under unreasonable impulsion from it. Guidance is received because one simply opens themselves to receiving it. Our place in the cosmic order is to act as a distributor of this divine power.

This is evident in physics whereby we never create force; all we do is re-distribute it. Hence, this is proof enough that Source is flowing through us all the time; all we need do is learn to become an effective distributor of its power. At first the path may feel narrow and humble. However, over time you will discover the flow begins to grow wider and higher. This is because it is the nature of LIFE to continually EXPAND because Spirit is infinite. It KNOWS no limits.

Source exists as an infinite supply that is giving, non-judgmental and all knowing and shows us that we are loved. Source in and of itself is the ultimate Principle of INCREASE as it grows in and out of our present conditions because it is an expansive energy. To connect with Source, all you need to do is make a sincere effort to let go and allow for a strong clear connection to it. Your soul intuitively already knows how to do this. All you need do is remember.

Consciousness arises as it interacts with Source Energy. Both Source and Consciousness are non-local, without form and therefore infinite. Hence, when one has a strong connection to Source, one can ask questions and receive solutions to any problems.

By establishing a sincere relationship to SOURCE it expands one's personal being because one ALLOWS oneself to experience a greater intelligence than their own to flow through them. This Intelligence is the very Principle of LIFE itself. ALL one needs to do is to simply become willing and OPEN to **RECEIVING** its energy.

Just as nature provides for us an infinite supply of beautiful colorful rainbows, it is impossible for us to have TOO MUCH because the universe we live in does not exist as a closed, limited system where only so much is available to go around. When you allow an extraordinary amount of money or

> Wise Words of Wisdom - Our connection to Source becomes weak when we believe that our mind is weak, impotent or fallible

supply to enter your life, you are merely completing this cycle. Universal Abundance by its very nature is limitless.

CHAPTER 5
EXPLORING THE FIELDS OF ABUNDANCE

Definition of Abundance - More than Enough

Abundance exists as fields of flowing energy that surrounds us at all times. This ENERGETIC FIELD impacts our health, relationships and finances. A lack or blockage in any of these, restricts the flow of this energetic field. Hence, abundance exists as an intangible field that greatly influences our surroundings. Did you know that mustard seeds are almost invisible to the human eye. Mustard seeds are small round seeds measuring between 1 to 2 millimeters. Hence the saying "*faith of a mustard seed*" because faith too is invisible, yet its results are visible if one remains patient. enough.

Like the good life, we are instinctively drawn to joy because of its inherent truth and beauty which is a vital component of abundance because as Spiritual beings seeking a higher existence, we are naturally attracted to the good life; to enjoy all life has to offer. The good life includes feeling safe, having peace of mind, a supportive family and a loving and fulfilling relationship.

The non-existent is whatever we have not sufficiently desired. To have more abundance, RECOGNIZE NOW the abundance that already exists in all things. Recognize the rainfall or water that nourished the plants to produce the abundance of fruits and vegetables or the abundance of bees that give us honey and makes the fragrant flowers bloom.

Wise Words of Wisdom - Celebrate and thank the good in your life if you want more good

Digging deeper into the definition of abundance, we see that affirming abundance is a mild act of gratitude and one discovers that abundance is in direct proportion to the health of one's social life, one's sense of self worth and the health of one's relationships. It is one of the few things in life that does not mind being taken advantage of. Take advantage of the fresh air, bright sunshine and all the abundance that exists in nature and allow these to inspire you. RECOGNIZE the endless varieties of fruits and vegetables at your local Farmers' Market. New businesses that are opening or the infinite number of websites that can be created. Visit affluent communities in your neighborhood and affirm the abundance of this earthly dimension is holy and good.

TIPS FOR DEVELOPOING ABUNDANCE CONSCIOUSNESS

* Visit a local Farmers' Market and RECOGNIZE the bounty of rich, fresh, delicious nutritious food, flowers and locally produced crafts.

* Acknowledge the growth of new businesses, their expansion and the owners' expectation of success.

* Recognize the trees and the abundance that exists everywhere in nature.

* Recognize the natural flow of cycles.

Thoughts of poverty and abundance cannot both co-exist together at the same time. Your consciousness gives rise to one of two types of experience - abundance or lack. Recognizing abundance and developing a keen awareness when thoughts of lack slip in.

WHY NOTHING CAN EVER BE 100% CERTAIN

Nothing is impossible because it can never be 100% proven that it will fail. Hence, anything that you think is difficult or impossible can never be 100% certain that it will fail, which is why new inventions always occur or are improved upon. A trick to get your attention of your subconscious mind to prove this is to ask questions. For example – ***"Can you be 100% sure that you are unable to afford whatever it is you want to purchase?"*** This same method can also be applied to fears. *"Can you be 100% certain that this fear is real?"* The opposite is also true, which is why insurance companies are such a success. For example you can never be sure your car is going to start 100% of the time, or your house will remain 100% free of leaks or your boat for that matter.

Ask yourself the following questions –

*"If I didn't believe it was possible to __________________,
what could I do today to take small steps that would put this into motion?"*

or

"If I didn't believe that I have to remain stuck in this position, what other options would be available?"

or

"If I didn't believe it was possible, than what could I do?"

SUMMARY

Simply acknowledging and recognizing the abundance that is already in your life, lays the foundation for experiencing more. Abundance can become a state of mind, if one learns to RECOGNIZE existing abundance. Because the universe responds strongest to feelings, FEEL and experience the aliveness in the abundance that already exists all around you and you will effortlessly attract more of it.

Enjoying the satisfaction of having completed a difficult project reminds us of our infinite potential

CHAPTER 6
FEAR - False Events Appealing Real

Fear's response to a situation occurs as a protection mechanism. However the fact is 99% of all fears don't come true. Taking common sense precautions and / or allowing use of Intuition are all that is necessary to keep you safe.

When one dwells upon fear, the fear may end up manifesting. One trick to avoid this is to write out on a blank sheet of paper what you don't want to happen. This creates an emotional release because writing out something is a form of therapy.

Fear is contagious and has its own momentum. Anytime a fear comes true, you give it credit for its having protected you. Fear fools us into thinking we are not safe, which in truth really is pure illusion. Fear's purpose it make the illusion reality. The antidote to this is to learn to **live in the moment**.

Fear's power comes from when you give into it or when you allow it to fool you into re-visiting the past or experience an uncertain future. The secret is to learn to develop internal control so you can understand that fears are a direct response to an INTERPRETATION of external events or situations. KNOW that the world at large is not out to get you or is waiting to attack you for no good reason. This is a perfect example of a PERCEIVED threat. The most rapid way to dissolve fear is to **HAVE GRATITUDE** for all the good things in your life because fear and gratitude cannot co-exist together.

Transmute the power of fear by aligning your desire with the Divine. This allows your desires to FLOW TO YOU, rather than you having to go after it.

A neat trick to help you open up your mind to gratitude, is to imagine a square grid (*like those on a camera*) superimposed over a portion of your eye's vision. Don't move your head or eyes. Next look at each square

Wise Words of Wisdom - There is no faith without uncertainty individually and focus on anything you see that you identify as grateful for. Next do the same with the next square and the next until you have filled in all the squares. Next look at the entire grid and see the gratitude in all the squares.

Love and Profound Gratitude is the antidote to all fear because its high frequency is one of receiving. Visualize your heart aligning with your desire or thoughts of infinite abundance. Next imagine your heart merging with your thoughts and infuse the energy with gratitude.

REMOVING ONE'S FEAR OF SNAKES

Many people fear snakes. One neat trick to get rid of snakes or before you go hiking in an area that has a lot of snakes is to repeat the following with SINCERE INTENT – *"I Sincerely Respect the Spirit of the Snake and I beg its Pardon"*. You might want to burn sage smoke before repeating this phrase for extra potency.

RECOGNZING YOUR TRUE SELF WORTH

The first five letters of worthy are WORTH. Hence you have something of value to offer the world (your divine gifts and talents) and the world recognizes this value.

The success of a community is determined by the amount of compassion expressed by its inhabitants

HOW TO AVOID FEAR FROM SABOTAGING PROSPERITY CONSCIOUSNESS

We live in a period of unprecedented abundance and personal prosperity, where people have more access to the necesssities of life such as clean water, electricity and education and we see record progress being made each and every day with new innovations and technology almost on a daily basis. Yet, when we turn on the television and watch the main-stream news, we see poverty, lack and limitation. Why is this happening? As stated in the January 2015 edition of Scientific American (*page 78*) our brains make up 2% of our body weight and consume 20% of the energy used by our body. In today's modern world our brains are still wired for survival. Hence, specific parts of our brain are still easily stimulated by outside influences. These parts of the brain can overwhelm our emotions, one of which is fear. Even if the fear is not a threat, we still have a tendency to go into "***survival mode***" out of pure primeval instinct. The main part of the brain that becomes stimulated when fear is experienced is the Amygdala which is circled below in the picture shown on the left.

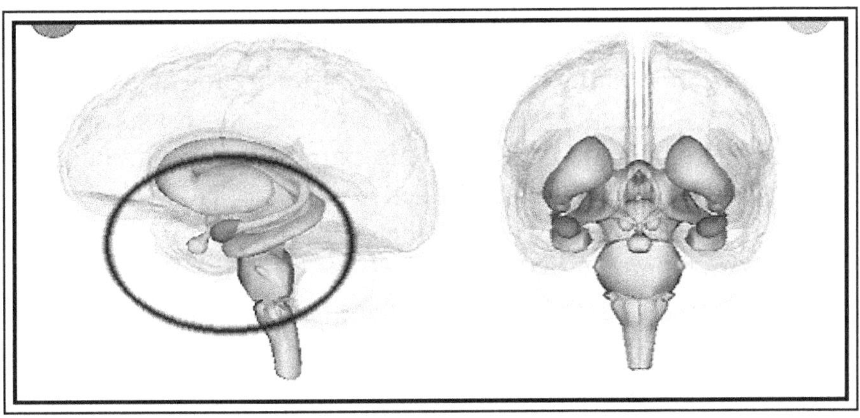

This is why some of us are still instinctively drawn to scary movies because the stimulation of this part of the brain makes us feel good due to the chemicals it releases when stimulated. Because our brains are still wired for survival in the wilderness, taking advantage of this part of the brain has not gone unnoticed by specific individuals who use the stimulation of the Amygdala for profit or for their personal hidden agendas by over exacerbating certain events and situations. Hence, because fear creates resistance, it can slow down your decision making and your ability to think logically.

Some, but not all, large media corporate networks take advantage of this fact. For the most part, this is because FEAR increases ratings, which in turn creates more profit or supports a specific agenda. The antidote to this is to learn to quiet and still the mind and learn to judge the truth for yourself based upon the answers that come from within; especially the heart. Our hearts know what is authentic and what is not authentic; one just needs to learn to exercise their "*inner authentication radar*" when reading or watching the news.

One tip to connect with your inner authentication radar is to become knowledgeable, self-educated and to skillfully seek out reliable information sources. As our world becomes more interconnected and the sharing of information grows, more and more people will learn to define what is truth and what is designed to only increase ratings.

The human race is trying to evolve to a point where emotions don't overwhelm logical thought and reasoning. This puts us in the position today where our technology has evolved faster than our biology. For some of us, our brains are still sensitive to primeval fears. This part of the brain becomes stimulated when perceived danger is present. This is called the **Fight or Flight Syndrome** and there is also scientific evidence starting to confirm that this response also accelerates aging.

In the United States today, too much emphasis has been placed on healthcare, causing some people to lose touch with this important connection. When one can learn to listen to the inner messages their body is telling them (*intuition*) one can not only determine between fake news and real news, but also take wise and prudent steps to remain fit & healthy.

Fancy Fact - The first few minutes upon waking up, the mind does not experience thoughts of fear or lack, but is in a neutral state of mind.

FACTS ABOUT FEAR

- Fear of success is similar to the fear of failure

- Fear impairs judgment and also stagnates action

- Discomfort can move you out of the zone of fear because it forces you to focus on the next task. Hence the saying necessity is the mother of all invention.

- Consistent ACT-ion dispels fear because a habit of new behavior overwrites feelings of hesitation

- Fear of Rejection. Stems from fear that exterior influences are necessary to make you happy

If we can't accept the pain that comes with changing our thinking, then one forfeits their intelligence. If one wants continued personal and professional growth and success, one MUST learn to tolerate the discomfort that comes with it. For example, a person who lifts weights knows the size of his muscles are increasing whenever he feels the burning sensations occurring in his arms or legs.

Success is the progressive realization of a worthy ideal realized

CHANGE IS THE ONLY CONSTANT

The only constant is change, which is inevitable. Change has the power to re-define our purpose. The only constant in the universe is change because everything down to the smallest atom is vibrating. Hence, the bigger the change, the larger the vibration and the more intense the emotional discomfort experienced. When changes happen faster then we can keep up with them, knowledge can be a great tool to help one cope. Take time every few months to take a break and review new technology, new ways of doing things and ways you can economize and delegate your tasks and responsibilities to save you time and effort.

EXERCISE #1 FOR NEUTRALIZING FEAR

People accept, surrender and believe thoughts that are equal to their current emotional state of mind. Catastrophizing your fear is remarkably effective in alleviating fears. First explore, by writing out, or saying out loud the worst case scenario that could happen; the very core of the fear. This one simple technique reduces the emotional arousal caused by the perceived threat because it has the unique ability to create a barrier from the perceived fear by intellectualizing the fear, rather than through fear based emotions. Over time one will discover that fears really are an illusion and that situations are not all that difficult as they appear to be.

EXERCISE #2 FOR NEUTRALIZING FEAR

Imagine a scale going from 1 to 10; with 10 being the most intense. Next ask yourself - *"How likely is it that the thing I am fearing could ACTUALLY come true?"*

SUPERSTITION BREEDS FEAR

Some people believe fate is controlled by magical behavior. Superstitious behavior comes from a fear of failure and a person's lack of confidence in themselves. Some people use superstition as an excuse to avoid personal responsibility.

If momentum caused by fear has sabotaged your dreams, REALIZE that you can swing the momentum BACK your way by paying attention to your awareness and how you feel. Know that the choices you make at this very moment will dictate the days ahead.

Wise Words of Wisdom - When one learns to intellectually rationalize their fears, fears become greatly diminished

WHY DECISIONS BASED ON FEAR FAIL OVER THE LONG TERM

Fear creates illusions which wall us off from our inner wisdom. Because fear = resistance, any decision made out of fear will only create a momentum of lack over the long term. This is because the state of consciousness that created the problem can't solve the problem because the same state of mind exists.

FEAR OF FAILURE

Our souls exist within us so that we may learn through mistakes and awareness so we may more abundantly contemplate nature's divine power and wisdom. All failures are designed to serve and help you learn. Many people don't follow their dreams simply because they are afraid of failure. The truth is how do you know you will fail if you don't even try? Ask yourself this, " *Will I still have my needs met if I pursue this and I end up failing?"* If the answer is yes, the fear is false. Ask yourself again, *"Can I still love myself during the process as I pursue this?"*.

The amount of change that is able to take place is in direct proportion to the amount of fear you may experience. The bigger the change or situation, the bigger the sense of fear (which is illusion). Hence, to keep winning and losing in perspective, don't think about either one.

Mistakes are valuable because they teach us that we are responsible for our own internal happiness. It is a learning process to learn to see failure as being part of the process of acquiring your goal or desire. In retrospect, there is no such thing as failing at anything because there are always possibilities that manifest in the interim. For example –

Wise Words of Wisdom - Fear of Failure comes when one strives to prevent the very changes that will abate it.

> ➢ You are on your way to work and you come across a detour. You take the detour and happen to drive by a beautiful forest with a lake and stream that you have been dreaming about for years to visit.

> ➢ Another example is you have spent days preparing for the perfect wedding, only to have a sudden thunderstorm occur on the wedding day and you had

to cancel the live band. Instead you hold the wedding indoors in a small building and decide to turn on the radio. While listening to the radio, you learn that the first three callers to the radio station will win a free trip to the British Virgin Islands. You call and discover you are one of the first three callers. So, instead of getting frustrated, RECOGNIZE the alternatives and possibilities that are showing up and without hesitation CAPITALIZE on them.

SUMMARY

No amount of energy put towards preparation of any project, large or small goes un-rewarded. As long as you ACKNOWLEDGE this one simple fact and open yourself to the possibilities that present themselves, you will ALWAYS be rewarded with positive unexpected outcomes. In retrospect failure is fertile ground not only for a strong comeback but for one to experience the alternative positive opportunities.

Detours or unexpected events that pop-up unexpectedly after extensive planning is the universe's way of teaching us or showing us things that we might not have noticed before because this is the only way it can get our attention. This is because we don't always know what is good for us, but the universe always does. So the next time something unexpected occurs, such as a detour, or something does not turn out as planned, look for the alternative good that is revealing itself, and celebrate its unexpected appearance. because it may turn out to be something better than you had originally expected!

Did you know – Two of the most profound discoveries, penicillin and dynamite were discovered solely by accident?

Law of the Universe -
You have no control over exterior events or circumstances, but you DO HAVE **FREE WILL** over how you **RESPOND** to unexpected events and circumstances.

Competitive Aggressiveness

Tentative or submissive actions come from fear of failure. No absolute will ever make a lion lay down next to the lamb unless the lamb is inside of the lion. The synonym for aggressiveness is assertiveness. There is a time to be nice, caring and cordial and a time to be aggressive. Don't fall into the trap of being nice out of a sense of feeling powerless. This allows those around you to plunder your spirit to enrich themselves.

History has shown that in competition, it is the aggressive competitor that has more of a chance of success because their aggressive approach intimidates the competition by confrontation. Aggressiveness in competition must be balanced, controlled and positive with forethought because excess aggressiveness leads to the Bull in the China shop situation. There is a time to play warrior and a time to play gentleman.

The Dark Side

We all intuitively know about the "dark side" just as we know about the "light" and are able to intuitively connect to it. The dark side is bound by its insecurity and shortcomings, hence the best advice is to avoid it as the dark side cannot destroy what it cannot see. Most of all do not glorify the dark side or allow yourself to become overwhelmed by it.

CHAPTER 7

LEARNING TO MANIFEST USING 5TH DIMENSIONAL ENERGY TECHNIQUES

I want to start this chapter with selected lyrics from the song Flashdance.

Take a hold of my heart - What a feeling - Bein's believin' - I can have it all - Take your passion and make it happen - Pictures come alive - You can dance right through your life!!

5th Dimensional Energy is all about working with the Heart. By learning to create using the 5th Dimension, your desires flow TO YOU. Is where everything is simultaneous or all happening at the same time (ALL IS ONE). This is because manifesting from the 3rd and 4th dimensions there is disorder. You may still get what you want, but it is going to be a struggle. Energy in the 5th dimension exists as beauty and magnificence which permeates the 5 senses. There is order, perfection and everything is complete.

Desires are experienced differently here. Instead of material things, one recognizes qualities, virtues, goodness and purity. Hence, these are qualities where real manifestation springs forth from.

The first step is to believe on a subconscious level in your own power, including the power you can create positive, loving and abundant changes in your life. This will greatly speed the process of manifesting what you want.

5TH DIMENSION CREATION EXERCISE #1

Use this exercise to heal any past trauma, inadequacies or deplete old energetic patterns. It is also a great exercise to generate feelings of contentment.

1- Place your hand on your heart and hum.

2- Imagine you are placing that hum inside your heart and allow your consciousness and physical eyes to drift towards your heart.

3- Next imagine any past event that has you stuck in the present or is causing pain and place it in your heart as you continue humming.

4- Allow the beating of your heart and humming to transform the past trauma.

5- Next imagine the past event transformed into a bright light, gradually expanding outwards from your heart, until you can't see it any more. When you can no longer see the light, acknowledge that the past experience is completely healed and no longer a part of you. Any memory of it only returns to the brightest glow of white light in your heart.

CREATING USING THE 5TH DIMENSION. EXERCISE #2

Thoughts are electric and feelings are magnetic. How do we combine the 2 to manifest our desires? Magnetism generated by the heart's coherent field creates its own magnetic energy and the power of intention is carried upon that energy. This generates a new frequency that is broadcasted into the quantum field. Hence, you no longer have to put out excess amounts of energy / strive / frustration to achieve something. Space and time collapses, drawing experiences to you. A new vibrational match now exists between your energy and your desire. Through repetition, this quantum magnetic field gets stronger and stronger. You can use this technique for healing, to obtain a new job, attract new opportunities, experience mystical experiences and more. The key is to begin small until you are confident enough to move onto the big stuff.

1 - Write down on paper your intended future financial goals for the next 3 to 6 months.

2 - Next contemplate on Spirit and allow Spirit to reach DEEP DOWN INTO THE DEPTHS OF YOUR HEART.

3 - Next FEEL and allow heart energy to flow out of your heart, energizing the intentions you have written down on paper.

4 - Next see your intention(s) written down upon the paper becoming fully aligned with your heart.

5 - Next see and allow the energy to manifest into form.

4 - Next allow this energy to merge into ONE.

5 - Over the course of the next 3 to 6 months, at various times contemplate upon the Spirit related to your financial goals.

Because the heart utilizes energy related to the 5th dimension, aligning your heart with intention DRAWS TO YOU your desire, rather than you having to "chase after It is a fact that our hearts emit a magnetic field.

SUMMARY

Clear Intention + Coherent Heart + Coherent Thoughts = Raises your vibration

WHY FEELINGS ATTRACT CIRCUMSTANCES

Life responds to feeling; the stronger the feeling the more life will generate an experience to match that feeling.

For example, we have all heard stories of athletes who used visualization to become better at their sport. This is because visualization connects one directly with their true feelings. Hence, the more feeling you put into something, the more life will respond in-kind.

If you say to yourself "*Oh I hate my job*" and you quit and you get another job, it won't be long before you also have your new job. The only antidote to this is to find what you truly LOVE to do, what inspires, desires or motivates you. Only then will you find life SUPPORTING you because your feelings are now aligned with what you **LOVE**. You will instead find excuses to succeed rather than making excuses to tolerate what you hate.

While on the job, ask yourself " *Who am I becoming?" * or *"What is this job turning me into?"*

BE HONEST WITH YOUR TRUE FEELINGS

Just as we sometimes forget our connection to Divine Source, we may sometimes ignore our true feelings by seeking methods of escape. This is because our ego likes what is safe and familiar. So when we feel uncomfortable, the ego causes a separation from our true self, fearing a loss of the familiar. Feeling safe is a natural human instinct. However if you are 100% certain that a situation is not a threat and you want to see your dreams manifest, your ego is never going to be there to make it happen. The fact is change cannot occur without a change in how you feel about something.

HOW TO USE THE HEART TO ACCLERATE MANIFESTATION OF YOUR DESIRES

When one uses their heart to manifest, one receives what they asked for in greater measure and receives unexpected surprises along the way. Using the heart to manifest takes practice at first, because over time, just as an athlete has to practice using his or her muscles to stay fit, learning to align your heart with your intention takes practice.

WORKING WITH THE EXPANDED ENERGY OF THE HEART

1 – Allow your conscious awareness to gather around your heart.

2 - Hold some money in your hands and smell the money.

3 - Next see the money merge with your heart while repeating

for seventeen seconds - "***I am one with a tremendous amount of money***".

4 - Acknowledge your heart's ability to draw to you through the outer world that which you desire.

This technique has worked very well for some people when they want to manifest money quickly because the asking comes from being aligned with the Divine.

LEARNING TO MERGE YOUR HEART WITH YOUR FEELINGS

When one learns to live from their heart, one lives from a space of pure light and love which creates ease and peace. When the heart is open, intention is expanded which opens doors to the creative   subconscious   mind.

Working with our hearts requires one to relinquish control of their stubborn ego. Because our intentions are associated with feelings, when one merges their heart with their feeling it expands the intention significantly. The more positive the feeling, the stronger your connection to your heart.

HOW TO ALIGN YOUR HEART WITH YOUR DESIRES. A SIMPLE   METHOD

1 - Begin with a clear intention.

2- Next allow your heart to RECOGNIZE your intention by seeing your intention in front of your heart.

3 - Next imagine your heart and the FEELINGS associated with it.

4 - Next imagine your intention merging with the feelings of your heart into a single form of energy.

You will soon discover that your feelings related to your intention have changed. This is a positive sign that you will now start receiving impulses that will guide you towards your goal.

Just like a muscle needs constant exercise to keep itself strong, it takes practice to master the art of heart aligned intention. You may have to practice every day at first, but over time it becomes as natural as breathing.

There is an interesting correlation between our feelings and magnetic fields. A magnet is created by aligning its atoms with one another by using a strong magnet. When we align our heart with our feelings, they attract to us our desires.

In a research study published by Rollin McCarty and colleagues in March 2012 titled: *The Global Coherence Initiative: Creating a Coherent Planetary Standing Wave*, the authors state that using SQUID-based magnetometers they discovered that the magnetic field produced by the human heart is more than 100 times stronger than the magnetic field generated by the brain. This field is so strong it is able to be detected up to 3 feet away and extends outward from the body in all directions.

Fancy Fact - Our brains consume 20% of the energy used by our body, yet make up just 2% of our total body weight
(Scientific American . January 2015. page 78)

SUMMARY
Aligning our heart with intention changes our feelings, which in turn attracts to us our desires.

Wise Words of Wisdom - The stronger your purpose, the less interference you will encounter whilst pursuing it

HEART ALIGNMENT TECHINQUE #2

1 - Picture your goal or objective. See it surrounded with heart energy and filled with love.

2 - Allow the energy of your heart to absorb your intention, becoming ONE and experiencing it as if it was already a part of your life.

Even though your desire does not yet

exist, simply being at one with your desire clarifies your intention and by infusing it with heart energy, creates the necessary expansive energy for drawing your desire to you like a magnet.

WHY DESIRE ATTRACTS THE GOOD LIFE

When you find what you love doing, you have discovered your life's purpose. However, it takes a firm commitment to follow through on this at the very beginning. A desire that is followed through with courage is the best way to prosper long term. Take some time to explore what your true desire is. What

A clear goal solidifies purpose, leading to feelings of satisfaction

gives you joy and lights you up without effort. It is this effortless flow that creates the energy for you to prosper.

Satisf-ACTION

If you look at the word carefully, you'll notice that the last 6 letters spell **ACTION**. Hence; satisfaction is the reward for having taken action that propels you over the hills of life's challenges. Taking the time to acknowledge and reflect upon how much you have grown over the course of a year creates feelings   of   satisfaction   and   fulfillment.

Because energy creates, you receive a rush of energy from successfully   creating   something.

If you are a contractor, gauge the type of work that comes across your desk on a satisfaction scale from 1 to 10, with 10 being the highest satisfaction rating and aim to fulfill contracts that give you the most satisfaction. A simple example is shown below -

1 - Write down on paper a list of 10 things you love doing.

2 - Next assign these a satisfaction rating from 1 to 10, with 10 being the highest or the thing that

you love that gives you the most satisfaction.

3 - Using the top 3, create a bold plan of action to take you there.

CHAPTER 8
LEARNING FROM THE MISTAKES OF PEOPLE WHO HAVE LOST IT ALL

"If wealth & honor make you haughty, you bequeath misfortune upon yourself" -Tao Te Chin. Lao Tzu.

TYPES OF MILLIONIARES

> - **Pentamillionaire** - A net worth of $5 million.

> - **Decamillionare** - A net worth of $10 million.

> - **Hectamillionaire** - Ultra-High-Net Worth Individuals with a net worth of more than $100 million.

Just as some people look after their health and body and then purposely let their health go into decline through an unhealthy lifestyle, lasting wealth works the same way. Some people may spend years attaining a fortune than through a lack of awareness allow their fortune to also go into decline.

There are numerous stories about people who become successful financially, then suddenly and unexpectedly overnight lose it all. Some people, but not all, include lottery winners, inheritance money, lawsuits, sports stars and celebrities. These people may lose their money multiple times Why does this happen? The primary reason is their mindset. There may be erroneous beliefs about wealth formed during their early childhood. When they suddenly receive a large financial windfall they may fail to make the right investment choices or develop a scarcity based mindset that fears losing everything. Over time the ego, which wants to stay in control, leads to the mindset of *"I have all this money, I no longer need to have appreciation or gratitude for it"*. It is this *LACK OF*

APPRECIATION, for what already is, for having enough money, that eventually causes one to create a habit of subconsciously dismissing it from their lives.

Lottery winners who spend all their money within a few years are an excellent example of a lack of abundance mindset. I know this first-hand because many people who win the lottery move to Hawaii. When people play the lottery, they do so because it is gambling which is not based upon an abundance mindset. When they finally do win however, their lack of abundance consciousness causes them to spend, spend and spend some more until there is nothing left. The only people who make money and are able to keep it, are the people who have developed an abundance mindset over a period of years. Hence, these types of people invest their money wisely, adhere to a budget plan to watch their expenses and are vigilant about thoughts that lead to lack. Buckminster Fuller said that if all the wealth of the world's richest people was to be divided amongst all citizens of the planet, it would all soon be back in the same pockets.

When one works hard to create something it makes one see the value in what has been created. Hence, people who suddenly inherit or receive large monetary sums of money immediately, can't see the value in it. One antidote to this is to put the money away for a period of time, and continue on with life's routine. This allows ample time for one's wealth vibration to rise and adjust.

LITTLE KNOWN FACTS ABOUT MILLIONAIRES

* The term "***millionaire***" was first termed by Frenchmen Steven Fentimen in 1719.

* The average millionaire has declared bankruptcy at least 3.5 times [7].

* Four of the world's youngest billionaires are connected with

Facebook (*Sean Parker, Mark Zuckerberg, Eduardo Severin, and Dustin Moskovitz*) [6].

* The fastest growing number of millionaires are occurring in the following countries - India (21%), China (16%), and Singapore (14%) [9].

* Approximately 7% of U.S. households are millionaires [7].

* A 2010 study found that U.S. millionaires (those in the top 1%) pay about 40% of the taxes [4].

* In the book **The Millionaire Next Door**, 20% of millionaires inherited their wealth with the remaining 80% having earned their first million on their own [7].

* As far as type of car, most millionaires prefer a Ford followed by Cadillacs and Lincolns. This is because many millionaires avoid high-priced cars (unless they are ultra-rich) because economical wheels are investments that have little return and low maintenance costs [10].

* The majority of American millionaires are manager-owners with approximately half being self-employed [10].

* Carlos Slim Helu lives in a modest home and has a net worth of over $69 billion, earning almost $30 million per day [5].

* Approximately 80% of millionaires are college graduates, and approximately 18% have a Master's degree; 8% have a law degree, 6% have a medical degree and 6% have PhDs of varying subjects [2].

* First-generation Americans are more likely to be self-employed. The longer the average immigrant lives in the United States, the less likely they are to become self-made millionaires because they become accustomed to a lifestyle of high-

consumption [7].

* Just 20% of millionaires are retired with the remaining 80% still working [7].
* 17% of millionaires or their spouses attended private elementary or high schools. However, 55% of today's millionaires' children have attended or are attending private schools [7].

* Approximately 80% of American millionaires are first-generation millionaires [7].

* The fortune made by the first millionaire will have dissipated by the family's second or third generation [7].

* Russians living in the United States have the highest concentration of millionaires in America with the Scottish ranking second and Hungarians third. English ancestry groups rank fourth [7].

* Russian American millionaire wealth totals approximately $1.1 trillion (approximately 5% of all personal wealth in the United States) [7].

* Most millionaires do not live in mansions or in highly prestigious neighborhoods [10].

* Billionaire Bill Gates announced that he will leave a maximum of $10 million to each of his three children and donate his remaining wealth (estimated to be $61 billion) to charity [5].

* During 1900, there were only 5,000 millionaires in the United States, however by 2000 the number had reached 5 million [3].

* As of 2008, there were 10 million millionaires as classified in

U.S. dollars [9].

* Singapore has the most millionaires with 1 in 5 people being a millionaire, making it the city/state with the most millionaires per capita with 188,000 millionaires [9].

* In 2011, the number of U.S. millionaires dropped by 129,000 (approximately 5 million) [8].

* Approximately 1,226 billionaires exist in the world with women making up approximately 8.5% (167 women) [1].

* The average millionaire is approximately 61 years old with an average of $3.05 million in assets [6].

* In the United States millionaires are made up of the following job descriptions - managers (17%), educators (12%), corporate executives (7%), entrepreneur/business owners (6%), attorneys and accountants. Those in the $5 million+ group are made up of corporate executives (17%) and entrepreneurs/owners (12%) [3].

REFERENCES

1 - "Billionaires: The Richest Women in the World." Yahoo News. 2012. Accessed: December 26, 2012.

2 - Ellsberg, Michael. The Education of Millionaires: Everything You Won't Learn in College about How to Be Successful. New York, NY: Penguin, 2011.

3 - Frank, Robert. "Millionaire Population Grows by 200,000." The Wall Street Journal. March 21, 2012. Accessed: December 31, 2012.

4 - "Imposing Higher Tax Rates on the Wealthy Can Have Unintended Consequences." The Economist. September 24, 2011. Accessed: December 31, 2012.

5 - "Mesmerizing Facts about 10 Billionaires." Silicon India. October 12, 2012. Accessed: December 26, 2012.

6 - Palmer, Kimberly. "The 10 Youngest Billionaires in the World." U.S. News. June 4, 2012. Accessed: December 26, 2012.

7 - Stanley, Thomas J. and William D. Danko. The Millionaire Next Door: The Surprising Secrets of America's Wealthy. Lanham, MD: Taylor Trade Publishing, 1996.

8 - Tencer, Daniel. "Countries with the Most Millionaires." Huffington Post Canada. June 12, 2012. Accessed: December 26, 2012.

9 -. "The Wealth Report." The Wall Street Journal. April 11, 2012. Accessed: December 31, 2012.

10 - Tracy, Brian. Million Dollar Habits: Proven Power Practices to Double and Triple Your Income. Irvine, CA: Entrepreneur Press, 2006.

Jim Rohn, who was a professional door to door salesman and eventually ended up investing in Herbalife and later mentored present-day motivational speaker Tony Robins, talks about his early experiences as a younger man when he made over $3 million (during the 1970's) and then lost it all. He stated that the **ONLY LESSON** he learned from such a large financial loss was that when he re-built his fortune, that the only reason he was able to keep his money this time, was because he **CHANGED HIS INNER SELF**. He began cultivating an attitude of gratitude as well as made some other important life changes in attitude. This one simple step not only made him wealthy the second time around, but allowed him to keep his wealth.

A bad attitude is like a disease and needs to be dismissed as soon as possible otherwise it will grow, consume and destroy all the good works that the person has worked so hard to create.

Other people may view financial security as a substitute for their insecurity or previous experiences of poverty. Hence you can lose it all again because your vibration is one of lack, which attracts more of the same. The antidote to this is to not spend all the money at once, but instead gradually allow your body to adjust to the new vibration of having a large amount of money and learn to experience feelings of gratitude and appreciation for having it. Next take wise and prudent steps to invest the money so it generates a steady income for the rest of your life.

Did you know one person who has not lost it all is Oprah Winfrey? Oprah was the first U.S. African American woman billionaire and was the only African American billionaire from 2004 to 2006. What a lot of people also don't know is that she keeps a gratitude journal and swears by its effectiveness. What an amazing inspiration she is to all of us!!

Law Of The Universe - The human mind cannot have thoughts of both scarcity and abundance simultaneously

RECOVERING FROM A LARGE FINANCIAL LOSS

Remember that no amount of energy is ever wasted because the energy and effort you put into something creates its own unique blueprint of energy. The key to effortlessly re-acquiring lost wealth is to identify the blueprint of what already exists.

The larger the amount of money lost, the harder it is to get over it. Know that a large financial loss is a blessing in disguise because you really haven't lost anything. As long as the money that was created was created with an abundance mindset then the same mindset, blueprint and vibrations still exist and as long as you don't dwell on the loss that blueprint will still maintain its presence for a period of time.

Once you have acknowledged your loss, have appreciation for it and the lessons you have learned. The abundance vibration that remains within will slowly re-kindle **NEW DESIRE** within you. It is up to you to listen carefully and to follow these newly emerging impulses so that you may recover as quickly as possible. This re-kindling effect is natural and as long as you allow yourself to experience it, it will be the quickest way to recovery. Hence, you quickly fill in the financial blueprint that already   exists.

A neat little exercise to generate feelings of appreciation is to imagine yourself under a flowing waterfall consisting of pure appreciation. See the bubbles as the falling water hits the surface enter your heart.

How being Frugal Solidifies Long Term Wealth

The unnecessary wasting of resources is one of the biggest drains to wealth and prosperity there is. I remember reading in Dr. Wayne Dyer's Book No More Excuses how he would use toothpaste down to the very last drop. Unnecessary wasteful spending leads to one more easily dismissing money from their lives. Some of the world's richest people are also some of the most frugal. Warren's net is approximately $74.3 billion. In 1958 he bought a five-bedroom house in Omaha and has lived there ever since. This makes his home.001% of his total fortune. He does not waste money for no reason and just recently relinquished his flip phone for an iPhone and reportedly does not use a computer in his office (*CNBC. 5/22/2017. 7 Surprising Things in Warren Buffett's Office.*), (*USA Today. 2/25/2020 After Years of Owning a Flip Phone. Warren Buffett Finally Has an iPhone*). Warren also drives a Cadillac XTS, which he bought for $45,000 in 2014 (*CNN. 07/15/2014. "Warren Buffett Buys a New Caddy"*). Carlos Slim Helu, worth over 48 billion, lives in a modest home, drives himself around and avoids using computers. Also Paul Mitchell founder John Paul DeJoria, worth approximately 3 billion does not use e-mail or a computer in his office (*INC.com/magazine. June 2013. The Way I Work: John Paul DeJoria, John Paul Mitchell Systems*).

By learning to conserve where necessary and avoid waste it supports your road to long term lasting wealth. It is key however to wisely invest and spend on items that are necessary to further your well-being, keep you safe or help further a business. These investments will actually save you money and enhance your productivity over the long term

SUMMARY

* People who are grateful are far more likely to stay wealthy over the long term.

* True lasting wealth that continues to grow is always accompanied by personal inner emotional growth which is aligned with their belief system.

* Above average incomes come from people who have learned to become above average persons.

Gratitude is Good for Business

In the field of sales, gratitude has been shown to help contribute to long-term relationships between customer and company (*Bock DE, Stephanie MM, Folse JAG. The road to customer loyalty paved with service customization*), (*Esmark CL, Nobel SM, Bell JE. Open versus selective customer loyalty programmes. Eur J Mark*).

Consumer behavior studies have shown that gratitude in long-term customer relationships is the essential instrument for promoting customer loyalty (*Huang MH. The influence of relationship marketing investments on customer gratitude in retailing*), (*Prem PD, Sinha PK, Mathur S. Role of gratitude and obligation in long term customer relationships*).

Further Reading

What Role Does Patient Gratitude Play in the Relationship Between Relationship Quality and Patient Loyalty? Chih-Hsuan Huang et al. Aug 2019.

Gratitude and happiness: Development of a measure of gratitude and relationships with subjective well-being. Philip C et al. 2003.

Children Reflect Gratitude

A research study conducted in 2020 set out to determine if parents who appreciated their children's gratitude on a daily basis, if their children in turn expressed more gratitude. The study discovered that parents who engaged in gratitude socialization activity reported that their children exhibited more displays of gratitude over a seven-day period, in comparison to the control group.

Reference

Raising Grateful Children One Day at a Time. Andrea M. Hussonge et al. Jan 2020.

GREED

Definition of Greed - When a company puts profit above people.

Acts of greed are felt when people become harmed or injured as a person or company puts personal safety aside and focuses only on profit (*or in some cases negatively impacts the environment*). Hence the saying "*Profits before people*" or "*Greed is Blind*". Hence, greed is the result when a person or company has not yet taken the time to step back and take a look at how profit is made in direct relationship to a person's safety. These companies or people need to ask themselves "*Is my company (or I) negatively impacting other people or the environment as I make a profit?*" If the answer is yes, then if one continues down the same path, without accepting personal responsibility, there may be long term consequences. This could be why software companies are so profitable because their footprint on the environment is almost non-existent and the working environment is not as hazardous as compared to a mining operation.

For example, when automobiles first began to be mass produced, automakers ignored using safety glass for their windshields even though it was commercially available. Safety glass is glass that shatters into small tiny fragments so the person does not become shredded if they fly through the windshield during an accident. It was only after states in the United States began making safety glass a requirement in cars between 1936 and 1937, that safety glass was finally introduced into mass auto manufacturing.

There is nothing wrong utilizing the emotion of Greed to enrich yourself; as long as it does not harm another, your spiritual principals or greatly impact the environment in a negative manner.

SUMMARY

Some people who are wealthy have learned to master their mind in such a way that they get what they want without violating the rights of others. This is true lasting and long term wealth.

Can Money Buy Happiness?

Studies conducted by Di Tella and colleagues (*2010*) stated as income grows, one is half as happy after four years. Hence the effects of happiness related to income dissipate over time. This could be where the saying comes from "It is better to be rich and unhappy, rather than poor and miserable".

Income and Comparing Oneself to Others

In some individuals a process of comparison takes place in regards to income. Some people want to "keep up with the Joneses." Hence, they end up comparing their material possessions to that of their peers. In this case, increased income increases in one's income only lastingly raises one's feeling of well-being only if the former exceeds that of group income (*Diener et al. 1993; Clark et al. 2008*). This reason may in fact take the mystery out of why people don't seem happier (*not linearly*) as their societies grows richer.

The Effects of Societal Income Growth and Feelings of Envy

As a society grows more rich, it tends to become more unequal. Hence, individuals falling behind may experience feelings of deprivation. In turn, this can lead to feelings of negative emotions such as guilt, anger, envy or depression, decreasing their subjective feelings of well-being (*Subramanian et al. 2005; Wilkinson 1997*).

In some cases however, counterexamples exist where a person's subjective wellbeing grows rise with reference group incomes. However in these cases, the individual's well-being is due to a marked sense of altruism and community (*Knight et al. 2006*). In general, rises in income assist the poor to meet basic material needs. However as societies grow richer, relative income gaps and rising aspirations are expected to become more important in determining an individual's wellbeing than absolute income (*Diener and Seligman 2004*).

Reference
High income improves evaluation of life but not emotional well-being. Daniel Kahneman and Angus Deaton. Sept 2010.

Chapter 9
LEARNING ABOUT THE HABITUAL AND CONSCIOUS MINDS

The Habitual Mind (*also called the subconscious*) has been quoted by Norretranders (*author of* **The User Illusion**) that it processes millions of stimuli in our environment each and every second. The Habitual Mind is programmed early on in childhood and lasts throughout our entire lives. Thus, it is easier to learn a new habit then it is to break an old one.

Our brains show tremendous potential to process information. When a person is reading or piano playing, their brains are processing a maximum capability of 50 bits of information per second and our overall senses process approximately 11 million bits of information per second. However, the conscious mind processes only 50 bits per second.

The reason for this large "*Gap*" is partly due to the approximately half-second delay between the instant that our brains receive information and the instant that the human mind becomes conscious of the information

Reference: Britannica.com

Like a wandering glacier, 90% of our subconscious mind is hidden from our waking conscious mind. What's even more interesting is that the subconscious mind directs our thoughts and behavior (*the waking active conscious mind*) as we go about our daily existence on autopilot. Neuroscientist John-Dylan Hayes stated in the January 2015 edition of Scientific American (page 78) that our decisions are predetermined unconsciously a long time before our conscious mind kicks in. Hence, the ability to successfully re-program one's Habitual Mind can greatly leverage our ability to successfully accomplish our desires.

One interesting fact about the Habitual Mind is it reflects our current circumstances. For example, the amount of money in your life right now is a direct result of the amount your subconscious mind has been conditioned to believe it to be.

HABIT IS OSCILLATION

Oscillation creates frequency. An example of oscillation is the number of times it takes for one end of the pendulum to swing from left to right within a certain amount of time. Looking at this in the context of our habits, we can use the following formula –

HABITS = OSCILLATION = FREQUENCY = WHAT WE ULTIMATELY EXPERIENCE

In short summary, to change what one experiences one only need change their habit or routine (*oscillation*). This is because frequency can act as a receiver. Our subconscious mind is neutral. It does not know good from bad. Hence, what you consistently believe to be true, the subconscious mind will eventually see as real. Hence, if your subconscious mind believes that you have to work extremely hard to become wealthy, than life will create circumstances to support that belief.

Dwelling on thoughts of what you don't want or a lack of "*what is*" has already aligned some people's inner being with shortage and lack and asking for prosperity coming from this mindset will never manifest it. Hence, so much of wanting is about living in the space of what they don't have.

The next time you set out to achieve a goal, understand that feelings are associated with your desire. This is because the universe responds to feelings. When feelings of resistance are non-existent, emotions of who you truly are begin flowing freely, allowing you to experience enhanced powers of focused intention.

**When one has allowed themselves to expand their levels of openness, deservingness and allowing
they experience Quantum Leaps
of progress.**

When engineers design superconductors, the technology is designed in such a way that electricity flows great distances with the least resistance. This results in the electricity being able to flow long distances without losing any power.

> Resistance - When fear and doubt clog one's natural connection to the flow of plenty

> Allowing - A process whereby feelings of resistance fade away

THE DUAL POLARITY OF CONSCIOUSNESS
Your conscious thoughts are either in one of two states most of the time. These are Resistance and Hesitation or Love and Order. None of these two states cannot co-exist together at the same time. It is normal for our minds to switch between these two states throughout various times of the day. The switching of these two states of consciousness is responsible for the rhythm and movement in our lives. You can immediately find out which state you are presently in by becoming aware of exactly how you feel right at this very moment. Now let's take a look at **Wealthy Ken and Poor Joe** as examples of this dual polarity.

Poor Joe - RESISTANCE - FEAR OF WHAT HE DOESN'T WANT

Wealthy Ken - ALLOWING - LOVE - WHAT HE WANTS

Poor Joe asks for something because he is asking for it coming from a mindset of lack, excessive need or want. Wealthy Ken on the other hand does not ask, but remains open and allowing and knows deep down he is worthy and deserving of abundance. He then uses the power generated from this to feel that his desires have already manifested. By being in a state of allowing, wealthy Ken has learned to come from a position of faith and manifest, rather than from lack or necessity because there is no resistance.

Feelings of Faith and Uncertainty cannot both co-exist at the same time. Wealthy Ken has learned the art of aligning his intention with his heart, causing an attraction of his desire to flow to him.

One looses the need for want when they feel whole and content

SUMMARY

Eliminating the resistance (*although there is always SOME resistance*) of what you ask for speeds its manifestation when you learn to put your current circumstances aside and stand firm in your faith that you are already abundant.

Besides Wealthy Ken's technique, let's look at some other methods

Any goal immersed within the heart becomes energized resulting in changes in how one feels about their desired objective

A TECHNIQUE FOR GETTING INTO THE FLOW OF ABUNDANCE AND ELIMINATING RESISTANCE

1 - On a scale from 1 to 10 with 10 being the most fulfilled - Ask yourself the following question - *"How satisfied do I feel at this very moment in my RECOGNITION of abundance?"*

2 - If the number on the scale is below a 6 or a 7 proceed to step number 3.

3 - First observe and **RECOGNIZE** the abundance that already exists about you.

4 - Next allow yourself to let go and fully **EXPERIENCE** the FEELINGS of abundance.

5 - Now re-rate your feelings using the scale on how satisfied you feel in your RECOGNITION of abundance. They should now be above 7 or higher. If not, repeat the steps just shown.

If you are somewhere you can't recognize existing abundance, go some place you feel abundance is more obvious and recognize and experience it there. After doing this, next gauge your feelings of fulfillment on the scale from 1-10. They should have shifted and you will now find yourself in the natural state of **ALLOWING**.

As you begin to see that all abundance is equally valid, resistance dissolves and abundance flows because you do not have an attachment that causes you to single it out. Attachment hinders expansion because everything is constantly expanding. Detach from the distractions that occur around you. Commotions, like unnecessary fear take up your attention and drain you of valuable energy. Reacting to every little thing, unless it is for protective measures, squanders / wastes valuable energy.

Even though your desire does not yet exist, simply being at one with your desire creates an expansion its intention. By keeping the faith and aligning your heart energy with it, it will eventually manifest it as long as it is meant to be. By believing passionately in something that does not yet exist, you create the room for it to manifest. If you lose confidence in yourself along the

> *Small Minds discuss people. Mediocre Minds discuss events. Great Minds discuss Ideas.*

way, it will feel like the Universe is conspiring against you. However, by keeping faith in yourself it affirms your continued faith in the Universe.

If you are serious about earning more money or generating higher profits right now at this very moment, **BELIEVE** you are capable of making more then you have been making. Another tip is to re-evaluate your existing beliefs by writing them down on paper and determine if they are limiting beliefs. Ask yourself why you can't turn your monthly income into your weekly income or turn your yearly income into your monthly income. Have trust that the Spirit and the Wisdom that created you has given you the opportunity to explore the possibilities of your divine gifts and use them to overcome any challenges; **KNOWING** that the universe does not give you a challenge that is too big for you to handle.

The real key to not encountering limiting beliefs in the first place is to live your life based upon your true desire. Once you uncover your true desire and adhere to the principles necessary to mold it into a financial success, you will naturally have the joy and enthusiasm to make it become a reality. Over the long term, this creates wealth that can last an entire lifetime. It takes courage, fearlessness and persistence to follow your desire. However the journey is well worth it in the end.

Wise Words of Wisdom - Nothing in reality is either unpleasant or pleasant by nature; all things become routine by repetitive habits

Additional Tips for Supporting New Belief Structures -

- Self hypnosis
- Cultivating abundance awareness through thought awareness
- A willingness to form new habits
- Energetic Architecture Clearings. These are a type of

spiritual exercise (*see Chapter 23 for details*)
* Repetition
* Reciting out loud - "*I command my subconscious mind to* ___________. "

ASSISTING THE FLOW OF INCOMING MONEY
Before you receive a lump sum of money it can help to put the mind into a state of ease and allowing. In other words remove any resistance to attracting money before you actually receive it. This helps "*push through*" the streaming flow of money that is headed your way, making it easier to receive it.

USING THETA BRAINWAVES TO DEVELOP POSITIVE HABITUAL THINKING

Up until age 7, the dominant brainwave patterns in the human mind are theta, which happens to be similar to the brainwaves a person is in when they are in a state of hypnosis. Hence, self-hypnosis is one effective strategy to re-program the subconscious mind.

THETA BRAIN PATTERNS

Twice per day the adult brain exhibits peaks in Theta Brainwaves. The first time is when the brain starts experiencing deep sleep. The second time is when the brain is awakening from sleep. In summary, just before bed and upon awakening, our brains are most susceptible to hypnotic commands and suggestions. Use these 2 times of the day to listen to subliminal tapes, subliminal CD's or subliminal mp3's that reflect your ideal routine or habit.

HOW TO TELL IF A BELIEF SYSTEM IS NOT SERVING YOUR HIGHER GOOD

Look at your current circumstances. Are they one of pain or struggle? one of excess effort? Do you constantly self-sabotage yourself? etc. These are all clues you have limiting beliefs somewhere deep within your subconscious mind. Just remember, this book is not about changing your belief system, but rather to re-acquaint you with the laws of prosperity as defined by the laws of the universe. Hence, if you are not prosperous or meeting your financial goals, then you are not in proper alignment with the true laws of prosperity.

TECHNIQUES FOR ELIMINATING RESISTANCE

1 - Behold and Observe that which you seek in all things, no matter how small or insignificant it may be. For example, if you want to enter and win a beauty pageant, than take note of the beauty that already exists in that pageant. Watch a beauty pageant video and OBSERVE and take in all the beauty that exists. Silently affirm to yourself -

"I behold the beauty of all in this beauty pageant." When you acknowledge something, your thoughts take on the specific aspects and qualities of what you are observing.

2 - Examine any limiting beliefs you may have.

3 - Contemplate on what you want.

4 - Contemplating on Spirit, which creates the force to manifest what you want.

5 – Use creative visualization by mentally rehearsing what you seek.

The quote on the right is from Matthew in the holy bible. It simply means that when you allow yourself to behold what already is, you attract to you more of the same. The poor stay poor because their attention is constantly focused on lack which eventually becomes their dominant vibration.

Attr-ACTION = acting in spite of doubt or fear attracts to you your circumstances.

Quote from Proverbs 3 & 6

"*In all your ways* **acknowledge** *him and he will* **direct** *your path*".

WHY RETURNING TO THE FAMILIAR CAN BE FATAL TO PROGRESS

This is when the mind "**swings back**" to thoughts of worry, doubt, lack and / or limitation and it is entirely natural for it to do so. However, know that this is another opportunity to re-examine what thoughts are starting to form in your mind. This same oscillation takes place when you push a person on a swing and they go further and further up, creating the final overall frequency. When you feel your mind returning to thoughts of lack and limitation, know that you have been given an opportunity to "**swing back**" into a new set of thinking habits that are in-phase with your goals and desires.

Wise Words of Wisdom - The belief that your habits are going to be hard to change is only that, a belief

Law of the Universe –

You have no control over exterior events or circumstances, but you DO <u>HAVE A CHOICE</u> over how you RESPOND to life's circumstances

CHAPTER 10
WHAT IS POVERTY CONSCIOUSNESSNESS?

Adversity tests the true character of people by reducing them down to the level of their circumstance, or up to the level the challenge it presents. It acts both as a test and a stern teacher. True adversity allows one to become re-acquainted with their true self. A person's true character always reveals a person's true moral purpose because it exposes things a man chooses to avoid. Hence, if you want to know your true character pay attention to yourself when things are not going your way.

All hardships are opportunities in disguise, allowing one to perform at their best. They can create the greatest life changes. Situations that seem like hardship are really life's way of preparing you for the moment that yet is to come. The field of Human Consciousness is so tiny that when you immerse yourself in a challenging situation, your mind will tend to focus only on a single problem at a time. By allowing yourself to focus only on a strategy to overcome the challenge, you'll no longer feel the hardship or obstacles that come your way.

When an event or circumstance occurs that is beyond our control, it unveils our true potential because it forces us to rapidly find solutions. It is during these times we forget about our fears and reluctance.

We don't always get what we dream about, but we always get what we tend to tolerate or believe in the most. Make a conscious decision to no longer tolerate events, details or circumstances that lead to fear, doubt, scarcity or lack. KNOW that wisdom and knowledge can reduce hardship and new skills can increase your resilience.

Our finances have an ebb and a flow to them; therefore being broke is always a temporary condition unless one has contracted "*poverty consciousness*". Poverty consciousness also drains valuable time, feeling like nothing can get done. Have you ever witnessed extreme poverty? It is sickening and if you are around it long enough, you can no longer distinguish between what is financial abundance and what is lack.

Poverty, for those who make the choice to leave it, can be a blessing in disguise. This is because not only does one have time to contemplate a better life with all their spare time, but because when one chooses to shift their mindset to one of abundance consciousness, a tremendous vacuum is formed allowing one to experience what is commonly called "*a higher vibration or frequency*". Higher frequencies are always the dominant frequency. Hence, if one wants to shift their mindset to one of abundance consciousness, all one need do is use firm intent that it be so and make it a habit through constant repetition that avoids distractions.

Law of the Universe -
Nature Abhors a Vacuum

Poverty consciousness usually starts as a scarcity mindset, which includes thoughts such as - "*There is never enough time or enough money*". If this type of thinking continues, it develops into full blown poverty consciousness. If one wants to experience positive change, there must exist a power that exerts a greater effect than that of the current conditions.

Poverty consciousness can also be eliminated by temporarily suspending one's awareness of their existing circumstances while at the same time, focusing on their blueprint of future abundance. This often occurs when one masters the art of resilience.

Quote by Carl Jung - "*Our most important problems cannot be solved; they must be outgrown*".

WHY COMPARING YOURSELF TO OTHERS CREATES A FALSE SENSE OF SECURITY

Anyone from a developed nation can go visit an undeveloped country, look at the poverty and immediately feel abundantly superior. This act of comparison is pure illusion. Try visiting a prosperous region such as Beverly Hills or Monte Carlo, and see how you feel. By watching, listening and learning from mentors that are successful in their field, you end up comparing yourself to them. This comparison creates ambition, drive and the courage to aim for higher standards. Being around people who have similar goals and objectives in life rubs off on you in a positive way because you are in the right comparison environment.

Some people may think that being poor is Spiritual. A Spiritual person is more inclined to be wealthy because they abide by the principles of truth and honesty, building a firm reputation and business over the long term. Know that abundance in its own right is a Spiritual process because you come from God and cannot think of thoughts of lack or deceit.

TECHNIQUES TO RESTORING ORDER

Order generates security and peace of mind. A truly wealthy person has the ability to give and receive simultaneously because they have learned to master the art of deservingness (*allowing*). Any situation that unexpectedly appears they are able to adapt, and adapt to it quickly before it has the ability to overwhelm their resources. On the other hand, people living in poverty have energy fields that are contracted and disordered. Hence, the saying, to leave everything just a little bit neater than when you found it, honors order.

All solutions to any problem always occur in a relaxed mind; one of ease and allowing. Hence, the emotions of stress and relaxation cannot co-exist. Pain and stress in the body are the result of dis-ordered patterns that stem from your feelings, thoughts and ideas about how life operates. KNOW that you have free will and choice to remove old outdated patterns and learn to develop the ability to give and receive simultaneously.

HOW TO RESTORE ORDER WITH CYMANTICS

Nature is perfect in that it can create order out of chaos. One example of this is the emerging science of Cymantics which has recently been used to heal people. Cymantics is where a specific type of sound wave is played and as it is played, a highly structured order in the environment takes place. The order can be physically seen when the sound waves are played in water or on a thin flat surface layered with sand. When Cymantic sound waves are played, the grains of sand naturally organize themselves into highly ordered structures.

One way to rapidly restore order effortlessly is to simply listen to some Cymantics soundtracks. You will immediately find that after listening to Cymantics that you begin experiencing feelings of inner order and structure. This is because feelings of well-being are some of the highest frequencies in the universe.

As one **LIVES** in **PERFECT ORDER**, one **KNOWS** that one has become an expression of the Divine, ceasing strain and effort to compel action. One has become ONE with the All-creating Power which has a new ordered center from which to continue its creative spark and to seek a more perfect manifestation, through the conditions of cosmic order.

RESTORING ORDER WITH HEART COHERENCE

Another effective method that restores order to one's being is practicing the new science of **Heart Math**. Heart Math is a technique where a person learns to breathe in and out through their heart. Heart Math benefits include; less stress, a reduction in anxiety and numerous other health benefits.

Reference

Treatment of Anxiety and Stress With Biofeedback. Christine Dunster.   Sept   2012.

Because Heart Math uses the heart, one experiences at a deeper level who they truly are and what they are truly capable of. Hence, the benefits of Heart Math go beyond just health and feelings of well-being. The following technique I am about to share with you instantly neutralizes the drain that comes from some emotionally charged situations and turns it into positive energy. It can be done anywhere at any time and it takes only a few minutes.

A SIMPLE HEARTMATH EXERCISE

1 - Close your eyes and relax.

2 - Place your awareness around your heart.

3 - Now as you breathe in, imagine the breaths you take flowing into your heart. Try and imagine your breath is coming in and out of your heart space.

4 - As you exhale, imagine your breath flowing out through your heart.

5 - Imagine your breath entering your heart than swirling around your heart and then slowly going back out.

6 - Now let's add a positive heart feeling. Recall the last time in your life you felt good. A situation that filled your heart with happiness, joy or gratitude.

7 - Imagine yourself living that memory. Don't force it, just let the memory and emotions reveal themselves naturally.

8 - Next imagine these emotions shifting from your mind to your heart space, allowing the new positive emotions to be experienced in your heart.

9 - Continue breathing in and out of your heart and while you do so, continue recalling your positive past memory.

10 - To end the exercise, slowly open your eyes and return your awareness to your room or space. Try to continue on holding onto how you feel right now as you go about the rest of your day.

11 - Repeat as many times as you feel necessary until you feel like order has been restored.

USING THE HEART TO INCREASE ONE'S INTUITION
Intuition enhances the ability of the brain to receive and hold more information.   This is because one key to becoming intuitive is to let go of fear, anxiety, worry and similar emotions.

I would like to begin with a quote by Rollin McCraty in the research study titled: *Electrophysiology of Intuition: Pre-stimulus Responses in Group and Individual Participants -"we believe that intuitive perception involves the heart, brain, and nervous system's connection to a field of information beyond normal conscious awareness"*.

Research has found that the heart contains its own brain which is composed of approximately 40,000 neurons which act similar to neurons in the brain. Hence the heart has its own miniature nervous system.

Reference
Potential clinical relevance of the 'little brain' on the mammalian heart. Armour JA (2008). Exp Physiol 93, 165–176.

This shows that our heart, brain and nervous system work together in sync to give our brains information we use to make decisions. Could this mean that the information we receive also comes from the future? Let's take a look at the data.

Institute of Noetic Sciences senior scientist Dr. Dean Radin shared the results of a study he conducted. In the study, the participants' autonomic nervous systems responded in advance of seeing randomly selected pictures on a computer screen that were intended to elicit a negative or calming emotional response. The Heart Math Institute decided to create its own study, and added additional protocols to its study, including measuring brain waves (EEG), heart electrical activity (ECG) and heart rate variability (HRV). The study involved 26 adults. The participants were told the study's purpose was to test their reactions to stress. The volunteers sat down in front of a computer and were instructed to click a mouse when ready to start. The computer screen remained blank for six seconds, while the participant's physiological data was recorded. After 6 seconds a series of pictures was displayed on the screen with each picture being displayed for 3 seconds each time. Some of the pictures evoked strong emotional reactions while other images evoked calm emotions. After each picture was shown, the computer screen went blank for 10 seconds and then another picture was shown. This cycle was repeated for all 45 pictures

The study discovered that both the participants' brain and heart indicated receiving and responding to information involving the emotional intensity of the pictures *BEFORE* the computer randomly displayed the images on the computer screen; as if they were responding to a future event. The time line before their body responded occurred on average 4.8 seconds before the computer displayed the pictures. Most importantly of all, this study showed that the participant's heart received the emotions (information) before the brain received it. Rollin McCraty Ph.D. explained that the energy of the transmission first started in the heart, then went to the pre-frontal cortex part of the brain, ending at the stomach (gut).

Reference

HeartMath.com. A Deeper View of Intuition. August 26, 2019.

SUMMARY

The aha! moment we receive from inspiration emanates from our heart. Our heart is connected to fields of information not bound by the classical limits of space and time. This means true visionary leadership occurs within the heart and not the brain. And best of all, anyone has access to it. One simply needs the knowledge and awareness of how to access it.

Because the universe responds to our feelings, and our nervous system is connected to our feelings, this shows that practicing creative visualization, guided imagery or other mind techniques that allow one to imagine their ideal future, *"primes"* our nervous system to become in sync with our expectations, attracting to us our desires. Hence, the universe organizes events, circumstances and synchronistic behavior for us as the future unfolds.

Further Reading

Evidence for an anomalous anticipatory effect in the autonomic nervous system. Dean I. Radin

USING THE PLACEBO EFFECT TO DISSOLVE POVERTY CONSCIOUSNESS

A Harvard Study that was published in Psychological Science in 2007 found that a boring repetitive routine that was responsible for aches and pains was able to be transformed into something that was fun to do and in the process make one healthier. The study discovered that those who recognized their work as exercise, experienced significant health benefits. The study involved approximately 100 room maids that worked in various hotels cleaning rooms. When they were instructed to think of the cleaning of their rooms as a form of outdoor exercise, they lost weight over a 4 week period, showed a reduction of body fat and exhibited lower blood pressure. All this just because they changed their **AWARENESS** of how they felt about what they did on a routine basis.

Wise Words of Wisdom – God joins in when eagerness and willingness show up

Reference

Mind-set matters: Exercise and the placebo effect. Crum, Alia J., and Ellen J. Langer. 2007. Psychological Science 18, no. 2: 165-171. 2007.

This study showed that by changing how you perceive

something, that it can transform a situation of routine boredom into one of eagerness and fun.

DEVELOPING INTUITION

Intuition is learning to bring up information from deep within the subconscious. Learning to use your intuitive gifts is secondary; what is most important is what you learn from using your intuition; how it makes you a better overall person which is the most important thing.

Learning intuition is a structured process. The key is to learn to develop a healthy balance between structure and allowing room for the answers to arrive spontaneously. Intuitive information arrives at the conscious mind rapidly and it is key to learn to identify the small subtle impressions that contain the answers. Intuition can help you fill in gaps for missing knowledge. Fiction writers for example can greatly benefit from using their intuition. Working with your Intuition can help you fulfill your highest potential.

IDENTIFYING CHANGE

One technique to enhance your intuition is to become aware of small subtle changes in the atmosphere, the environment or surroundings. This is known as the **"ambiance"**. The secret is that as you do so, your intuition becomes more sensitive to small minute changes that occur in the atmosphere / environment that you want to explore. This allows your mind to read details in a higher contrast, which sharpens your intuition. You can use this technique to help you win playing cards because your opponents emotions change the ambiance of the atmosphere.

The key is to make yourself as sensitive as possible to the smallest changes in the environment. For example when you step outside into the street, the atmosphere is completely different. All the small changes create the overall atmosphere. In summary, find the small differences and question why these small changes are taking place.

The book titled: ***Drawing on the Right Side of the Brain*** written by Betty Edwards, was the original workbook used by the Military Remote Viewing Program named **Project Stargate**, as quoted by Lyn Buchanan in the interview titled: *Exercises to Cultivate Remote Viewing with Lyn Buchanan.* Remote viewing is the term used for developing intuition. The book is highly recommended for anyone that wants to sharpen their intuition.

EXPANDING YOUR CATEGORY INTERPRETATION

The average person has over 20,000 words in their vocabulary. The more words you have in your vocabulary, the better you are able to express your thoughts and your thoughts are what receive information from your subconscious mind, which is partly where your intuition flows from.

Let's first start with colors. Write out as many colors as you can, without looking at a book that lists every color. Write out all the colors until you can't recall any more colors. When you finish, refer to a book on colors and fill in the remaining gaps, writing down new colors. Next do the same thing with - Textures, Sounds, Temperature, Smells, Taste, Shapes, Sizes, Patterns and Positions.

Once you have your *category vocabulary* expanded, you will be able to project to a place or time and describe it in much clearer detail. You will find over time that you will become good at a single category. Some people are better at describing colors, other people describing textures etc.

When analyzing your results, avoid counting what you missed because it is impossible to describe anything with 100% perfect detail. Instead ask yourself - *"How well can I depend upon my intuition being right as I practice using it?"* or *"How better was this session compared to the last session?*

MAP DOWSING

This is a great way to avoid a lot of struggle. With map dowsing you can find *"hot spots"* related to the information you are looking for with ease. You can use this to find water, old mines or places of interest on a map. To begin =

1 - In your mind imagine a huge bonfire burning at the target location, representing the information you are seeking.

2 – Next say to yourself - "*When I pass my hand over this map, I am going to feel a hotspot that represents the target*".

3 - As you pass your hand over the map and you begin feeling a warm or invisible burning sensation, put an "x" at the location.

A similar method is used when one seeks underground water which is used to drill a well. One uses a fork shaped wire or wooden stick; holding the Y end with both hands. When one clearly states the intention – "***As I approach or are under flowing water, this wire will grow stiff and rigid, pointing down at the ground***". To find how many feet down the water is, one can ask the wire to sway or bend left or right with the number of sways representing the number of feet or have the wire tap the leg to indicate how deep down the water is.

CHAPTER 11
DEVELOPING EMOTIONAL RESILENCE

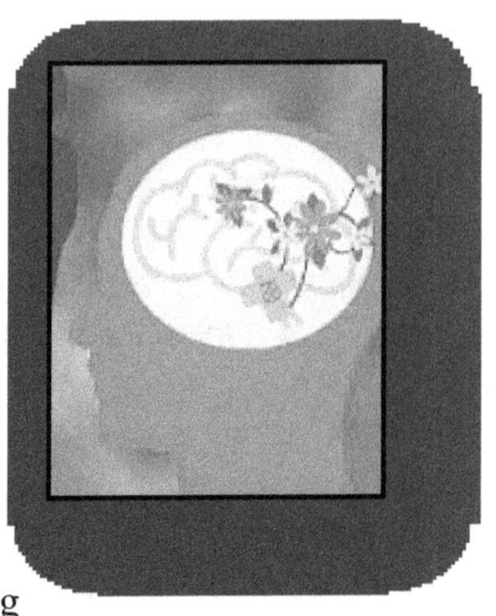

Besides re-programming your beliefs, one can measure their emotional response in regards to certain situations or environments. For example, if one has a past trauma they have not tended to or healed themselves from, just thinking about it can produce anxiety, doubt, worry or fear. Creating a strong Spiritual immune system affords you the emotional resilience necessary to deal with situations that unexpectedly arise.

Past traumas usually bring up emotions of fear. The more traumatic the situation, the more intense the emotion, hence the more dramatic the fear. This causes the self-repeating cycle of fear to be re-experienced through memory creating feelings of self-defeat in anticipation of encountering or expecting the same situation again in the future (*or similar situations*). If one can relieve these fears, it reduces anxiety in one's life. The Church of Scientology has used a device like this for decades and it is called an e-meter. Although you don't need to become involved in Scientology to eliminate your resistance or fear towards something, there are new technologies that can help reveal if you have emotional resistance towards something. The Emotional Freedom Technique has also been scientifically proven to work

References
Clinical EFT (Emotional Freedom Techniques) Improves Multiple Physiological Markers of Health. Donna Bach et al. Feb 2019.

The Effectiveness of Emotional Freedom Techniques in the

Treatment of Posttraumatic Stress Disorder: A Meta-Analysis. Sebastian B and Nelms J. Jan 2017.

A new invention has perfected E-meter type technology. The device measures skin resistance in regards to one's emotional state. This new technology appears to be more accurate than the ones currently available on the market today. The study found that the device effectively measures the emotional changes of a person in response to fear and joy.

Reference
A device for measuring skin resistance designed for emotional measurement. Sichen Xiao et al. Oct 2017.

LEARNING EFT FOR HAPPINESS AND HEALTH

Healing comes from feeling whole. Feeling whole comes from releasing internal emotional conflicts which cause one struggle. In some cases, this can be accomplished by practicing the Emotional Freedom Technique.

A study involving participants enrolled in a 4-day workshop that practiced the EFT technique, showed significant declines in anxiety (-40%), depression (-35%), posttraumatic stress disorder (-32%), pain (-57%) and cravings. The study also found that happiness increased (+31%, P = .000) and that the participants exhibited beneficial health benefits including healthier HRV (*Heart Rate Variability*). The study concluded that EFT improves a broad range of health markers across multiple physiological systems. These included significant decreases in pain, anxiety and depression as well as reductions in cortisol and a healthier immune system. Decreases in cortisol are associated with a wide range of health effects such as - increased muscle mass, enhancement of cognitive function especially learning and attention, increased bone density, improved skin elasticity and enhanced cell signaling. Most notably was the 74% reduction in cravings.

Reference
Clinical EFT (Emotional Freedom Techniques) Improves Multiple Physiological Markers of Health. Donna Bach et al. Feb 2019.

THE U.S. HAS THE HIGHEST SUICIDE RATE AMONG 11 WEALTHY NATIONS

According to a report by the private Commonwealth Fund Americans are the most suicide prone nation out of all the wealthy nations. The report also stated U.S. life expectancy is two years behind the 10 other wealthy nations.

CHAPTER 12
OVERCOMING PROCRASTINATION

Definition of Procrastination - The voluntary delay of intended action.

The Latin meaning of Procrastination means to '*put forward until tomorrow*". Everybody hates putting something off until tomorrow. In our daily lives we exhibit acts of procrastination in order to cope with negative feelings associated with specific tasks that we feel make us bored.

TIPS TO ABSTAINING FROM PROCRASTINATION

* Know that prolonged procrastination leads to negative self esteem.

* Know you will be worse off if you delay your intended actions. Delays due to life's responsibilities are healthy and normal.

* When you love and are enthusiastic about what you do, procrastination occurs far less often.

* Forgive yourself if you miss an important project. This will help keep your self-worth in good shape.

* Break your project down into separate pieces so you perform each task in a series of small steps.

* **ACKNOWLEDGE** that you missed doing something, than ask yourself the following QUESTION - "*What small steps can I take to get this project moving again?*"

* Know that by just **ALLOWING** yourself to get something started creates the spark to seeing a project come into fruition.

* Self regulation is a vital component to avoiding procrastination. Self regulation creates strength and must be built up and is exercised over time in order to remain strong, much like exercising the arms or legs creates strong muscles.

CHAPTER 13
OVERCOMING SELF SABOTAGE

We all self-sabotage ourselves to some degree. Did you know that the average adult thinks approximately 40,000+ individual thoughts each waking day? Hence, the same thoughts that you thought today will contribute to the quality of the day you will experience tomorrow. Negative self-talk can sometimes accompany these thoughts. Negative self-talk is a normal part of our thought processes, however sometimes it can become overbearing, leading to problems over the long term.

Negative self talk can also result in self sabotaging behavior, coming from a wounded ego. Negative self talk can also interfere with our plans to "*Think Big*", or "*Dream Big*". Hence thinking big is not going to make a difference if negative self talk is present. For example, thinking big when one experiences self sabotage will result in "*Big Expenses*", "*Big Bills*" and "*Big Debt*".

When you have learned to control inner negative self talk, DREAM SO BIG, you begin to think outside of the box and people begin to think you are crazy. The real antidote to negative self-talk is to become one in the moment and **KNOW** that these thoughts are not flowing from your authentic true self, which is loving and supportive. Learn to cultivate alert positivity. Another tip to break free of negative self-talk is to use meditation to quiet the mind.

TIPS FOR REDUCING NEGATIVE SELF TALK

- Listen to subliminal tapes before going to sleep or just before waking each morning. This programs your subconscious mind for prosperity consciousness.

- Know that it takes practice to change habits that have taken years to build up.

- Set a positive example by being an inspiration to others.

- Remain vigilant to thoughts that you feel are destructive.

Instead make it a habit to simply dwell on thoughts that feel good and that are in alignment with your goals / objectives.

Fancy Fact - One cannot hold a negative
thought for more than 17 seconds.

Tips For Eliminating Self-Sabotage

- Think of something you are grateful for and feel it in the present moment.

- Expect the best.

- Know you are worthy and **DESERVING** of all Life wants to give you.

- Re-align yourself with your desire.

Affirmation - My creative powers are in sync with the universe. I am the direct result of this power and intimately feel its connection.

THE VICTIM MENTALITY

We naturally create experiences in our lives in order to reflect our self-empowerment. When one becomes disappointed or encounters rejection, it can be easy to fall into the "*victim mentality*" trap.

Grief and its associated emotions come and goes in waves. Deep emotional traumatic pain which has arisen from a past traumatic event causes one

Wise Words of Wisdom - One can choose to stop tolerating unwanted circumstances by simply making a firm commitment to leave or make changes in their life.

to re-live the situation over and over when they think about it, leading to a victim mindset. Hence, one continues to manifest similar situations in their lives over and over (*the victim mentality*). The antidote to this is to learn to separate oneself completely from the trauma or situation. Realize that it is just a part of reality and learn to deal with it as best one can, then **completely let it go**. If this is not properly done, one will continue to re-live the incident over and over throughout their life; experiencing similar situations repeatedly. Besides the EFT Technique, the 5th Dimension Creation Exercise Technique shown in Chapter 7 can also help one release past trauma.

Summary

A victim mentality comes from re-visiting a past traumatic event. This causes one to attract to them similar situations because the past traumatic event has power over them because one has surrendered their power to the traumatic event.

KNOW that playing the role of victim does not suit one who is dedicated to overcoming obstacles on the way to their goal. See the victim mentality trap as a type of mental illness because it jeopardizes the quality of one's life. A victim mentality can generate a bad attitude, which is akin to a bad smell in one's thoughts. It takes personal strength and self discipline to avoid reliving past emotional circumstances which may cause one to blame people or circumstances. This can cause negative expectations to be put upon one from colleagues or friends. This forfeits a person's freedom because every human being has the freedom to change how they respond to their circumstances. Victim Mentality Frames of Mind include -

* Constant complaints about others come from wanting to Judge.

* Excessive thinking about revenge or painful experiences comes from past hatred and an inability to forgive.

* Excessive seeking out of enemies comes from a violent personality.

* Do you feel sorry for yourself?

* Do you complain, blame or make excuses?

* Learn to Create. You can't be a victim of you are creating with the co-creator.

UNDERSTANDING THE TRANSMUTATION OF NEGATIVE TO POSITIVE THOUGHT

Our thoughts behave similar to the way a tree absorbs nutrients from the soil, circulating it throughout its branches and leaves. Our mind cannot think a negative thought longer than 17 seconds because the thoughts that enter our consciousness are riding on waves of pure energy that eventually circulate through our consciousness.

GREMLINS AND SABOTAGE

When you make a firm decision to see a project through to full completion, your brain chemistry changes. As you work towards your goal or objective you may find that small disasters begin popping up here and there. For example, your car may suddenly break down, your computer may malfunction or an appliance may stop working. See these conflicts as an opportunity for you to work on alleviating them because they showed up and revealed themselves to you without any effort on your part.

The reason these "*gremlins*" appear is because instead of having only 1 purpose in life, there now exists a dual purpose which conflicts with each another. The antidote to this is to put forth sincere effort towards your new purpose, so your new purpose begins OVERWHLEMING your old purpose. RECOGNIZE that a conflict is occurring and raise it up to your awareness. Awareness is the starting point for efficacy, being the catalyst for transformation and change. If you have a mentor, continue seeking advice from your mentor asking for extra support. Once your new purpose outweighs your old purpose, and you have kept the faith, you will be free and independent of any future "*gremlins*".

Wise Words of
Wisdom –
Intention is the lens
from which the rays
of faith shine forth.

CHAPTER 14
LEARNING TO USE CREATIVE VISULIZATION EFFECTIVELY

What is Visualization?

Visualization is the act of mentally rehearsing a desired action which primes the brain in order to create a map to the future.

It has also been described as the method of recalling information in physical forms and images rather than in spoken language.

Visualization allows you to effortlessly teach your body emotionally what your future feels like ahead of actual future experiences. One example of this is feeling abundant in the moment and worthy in the moment attracts wealth to you.

Creative Visualization is called guided imagery in the scientific literature. Research studies have found that creative visualization can enhance physical performance in sports. One study published in February 2013 by Aymeric Guillot and colleagues titled: ***Coupling movement with imagery as a new perspective for motor imagery practice***, discovered that guided imagery improved the performance of active high jumpers when they spent time imagining their jumps before actual physical practice.

Additional References

Mental practice promotes motor anticipation: evidence from skilled music performance. Nicolò F. Bernardi et al. Aug 2013.

Effects of Mental Imagery on Muscular Strength in Healthy and Patient Participants: A Systematic Review. Maamer Slimani et al. Aug 2016.

Does mental practice enhance performance? Driskell, James E. et al. 1984.

Some people find they can learn to do a task better by using their imagination rather than by listening with their ears or vice versa.

Creative visualization works best performed up to 3 times a day in short intense sessions. It is most effective when one is about to perform a short term event preceding 48 to 72 hours into the future. This makes it perfect for athletes, actors, anyone preparing for a job interview or a large speech. In summary, using creative visualization up to 3 days before these events works   very   well.

Creative visualization can also help prove to oneself that working long hours to achieve something is an illusion. The famous golf player Jack Nicklaus claimed that before he hit each   golf   ball,   he   would   use   visualization.

When we learn to use creative visualization, we discover we have direct access to our nervous system and muscles. This allows us to better handle future experiences, allowing us to be more emotionally prepared as future experiences unfold. There is scientific evidence showing that our nervous system responds to an event before it takes place. Below are a few quotes from these studies.

Research Study 1

"Previous studies have suggested that the human autonomic nervous system responds to stimuli 2–3 seconds before presentation"

"The level of arousal of the autonomic nervous system, as measured by changes in SC, responds in advance significantly more before future audio stimuli than before future silent control stimuli"

Reference

Skin Conductance Prestimulus Response: Analyses, Artifacts and a Pilot Study. S. James P. Spottiswoode And E. C. May.

Research Study 2

"*demonstrating that the body can respond to an emotionally arousing stimulus seconds before it is actually experienced*"

Reference

Electrophysiological evidence of intuition: Part 2. A system-wide process? R. McCraty, M Atkinson, RT Bradley.

AN EFFECTIVE VISUALIZATION TECHNIQUE USED BY PROFESSIONAL ATHLETES

This technique comes from H.A. Dorfman, author of **Coaching the Mental Game**.

1 - The day before an important event or meeting, prepare your mind the afternoon before by visualizing what it is you want to see happen.

2 - Next, in the evening just before you go to sleep, spend the next 10 minutes rehearsing times you were at your best performance. For example, recall when you had your best day in - sales, athletics, academic performance etc. See and feel the times when you were at the absolute top of your game as if you were already re-living it. As you do this, you will discover that you end up falling asleep with these positive images playing throughout your mind and the next morning you'll wake up feeling confident, fearless and enthusiastic. You can also do step #2 up to 90 minutes before you put on your performance and it will also achieve satisfactory results.

METHODS THAT ENHANCE THE EFFECTIVENESS CREATIVE VISUALIZATION

When using visualization, see your goal as already existing in the present moment. Hold in your mind the image of what you want to manifest and allow yourself to experience new feelings, thoughts and sensations. Internalize the images until they resonate deeply with your inner being; **feel, touch, taste and**

experience what you desire as if it already actually exists in the present moment. Smell the smells, experience the textures, feel the sensations etc.

If you cannot hold in your imagination what you are visualizing, you will soon lose interest and fail. Learn to experience your sensory abilities through keen observation, recall and discovery. The secret is to use methods that holds your imagination's interest. Listed below are some of the best techniques -

1 - A simple exercise to get your powers of visualization flowing is to recall what you were wearing at your high school prom or the last time you attended a wedding.

2 - Learn to recall and visualize performances you had in the past where you succeeded. Experience the times you were "*IN FLOW*" and re-experience those triumphant emotions and feelings of joy, excitement and satisfaction.

3 - Add emotion to your feelings when you visualize your outcome. When emotions are merged with feelings it supercharges the imagination.

4 - Add the following when you use creative visualization to stimulate your imagination -

- **SEE THE COLORS** - Pictures on a wall, bed spreads

- **FEEL THE TEXTURES** - Curtains, door handles

- **SMELL THE FRAGRANCES** - Room freshener, freshly applied wood varnish

- **HEAR THE SOUNDS** - Accompanying sights and sounds

- **EXPLORE FURTHER** - Imagine DISCOVERING a gemstone in your bag. **FEEL** its texture, **OBSERVE** its size and *SENSE* its brilliance.

WHY LEARNING TO LET GO CREATES THE CLEAR PATH TO MANIFESTATION

It is key that one learns to let go after visualization so that the universe can go to work in manifesting it. Remaining too attached to the outcome can become a hindrance. I use the phrase -

"I detach, release, let go and surrender this work to my higher good, allowing it to fulfill its purpose as God and the Universe has intended it to be"

or

"Throughout the finished results of Christ another successful project is successfully completed now"

Also simply contemplating on Spirit as one nears the completion of a large project can help see it through smoothly.

Changes in the inner world of thought take time to be felt in the outside material world

Chapter 15
EXPERIENCING QUANTUM WEALTH

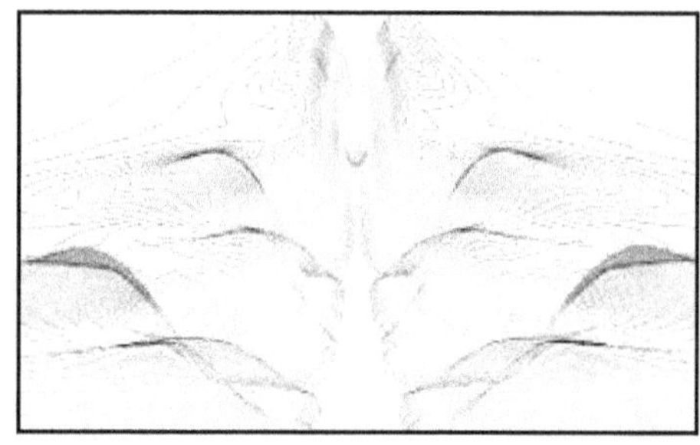

All things we touch and feel come from our feeling them at the subatomic level which exists in a hazy wave like state oscillating at high frequency. Beyond the hazy wave like state lies the solid physical state. Thus the reality we are experiencing now exists in a wave / particle duality. This hazy wave like state remains constant until we **DECIDE** to change it through the mere act of OBSERVATION. As we daydream, our dreams also exist in this hazy wave like state.

Quantum physics has proven that observing something changes it. For example, when a person has been **"OFFICIALLY"** diagnosed with a disease, the spread of the disease will usually accelerate at a much faster pace because the person now focuses and holds their attention upon it. The opposite is also true, one can train their mind to access the crests of these quantum waves through the simple act of Contemplation. The act of contemplating something penetrates the waves deeply enough in that as the waves rise, whatever the mind is contemplating on it, causes the energy in the wave state to change its form.

In order to turn our dreams into reality, such as money in the bank or coins in your pocket, you must sincerely convince yourself at the very core of your being that abundance IS NATURAL and that it is your GOD GIVEN BIRTHRIGHT because nature does not discriminate. Hence, by using guided imagery or creative visualization, you expect what you want to come into reality though feeling and experiencing thoughts and sensations that relate to your desire. You have now turned a daydream that once existed from a hazy wave particle like state, into solid physical particles in the physical material world.

CHAPTER 16
TIME MANAGEMENT TECHINQUES FOR ENHANCED PRODUCTIVITY

We have all heard the all-too common phrase *"Oh if only there was more time!"* or *"There is never enough time*!!" The fact is one can have more time when learns how time works.

TIME VS EARNING ABILITY

Let's take a look at time and how it can be used wisely to increase one's earning ability. For example, the person who has an online business, working 25 hours a week, making $35,000 a year and lives in Costa Rica is in an environment where the cost of living index is low. Compare this to the person working 40+ hours a week at the desk job in Manhattan New York earning $120,000 a year. The person at a desk job in Manhattan experiences high rent, high food prices as well as spending money commuting back and forth to work. Who is more prosperous in this environment? The person working 25 hours a week, or the person working 40+ hours a week? The person working 25 hours a week has learned to adjust his living circumstances in order to make better use of his precious time and in the process is better able to enjoy his life more.

Let's look at another example -
Poor Joe makes 25K a year for 40 years. He feels good because he made approximately $1 million over the course of that 40 years. However, Wealthy Ken is making $1 million a month. Hence, Wealthy Ken is approximately 480 times more wealthy than Poor Joe who took 40 years to make $1 million. Wealthy Ken has an abundance of time to enjoy his wealth. The difference between Joe and Ken is information and knowledge.

The more a person knows about a subject, the faster they can make money and the more time they have to enjoy it. Effective planning and preparation are ways to manage time. If you have ever spent some time in an affluent business district, you will always notice that time seems to flow differently compared to a non-affluent business district.

TIPS FOR MAKING BETTER USE OF TIME

> Keep a day planner and fill in the future dates with your tasks. Don't just put the day planner in your draw and forget about it. Carrying the day planner with you daily in your bag or keeping it on your desk at all times keeps you motivated towards your objectives.

Did you know that if you spent a few minutes at the region of the event horizon of a black hole, that months or even years can pass back on earth!

> Set time limits for specific tasks. Set a countdown timer with a set time limit, and give yourself a set amount of time to successfully complete the task. This works especially well for any task that is repetitive.

Did You Know? - If you smoked 3 packs of cigarettes a day for 46 years and instead reinvested that money, that the money over those 46 years could be used to create a portfolio worth over $2 million (*Tracy, Brian. Million Dollar Habits: Proven Power Practices to Double and Triple Your Income. Irvine, CA: Entrepreneur Press, 2006*).

Let's return to intuition again and explore it in a little more depth in the next chapter.

CHAPTER 17
HOW INTUITION WORKS

Allowing yourself to be open and ready to be guided by your intuition activates it. By being open you become immune to outside distractions, which helps one experience clear intuition. Whenever you start to make an important decision and you want to know if it is the right one, listen carefully to your feelings. Feelings of being rushed, experiencing a tight stomach, nervousness or restriction means that the decision you are considering making may not be right for you at this time. Asking questions establishes a direct link with their subconscious.

THE BEST INTUITIVE EXERCISES YOU'LL EVER FIND

These are techniques designed to get you in touch with your intuition. I have found them to be extremely accurate over the years. In summary *"intuitive hunches"* that you feel will be divided into 2 categories; correct and incorrect hunches. The emotions that accompany these hunches are shown below -

- ➢ **Correct Intuitive Feelings are** - Open, Light, Softening, Relief, Warm, Knowing, Confident, Trusting, Calm, Neutral, *"in the flow"*, no overbearing physical sensations.

- ➢ **Incorrect Intuitive Feelings are** - Heaviness, Tightness in Chest, Uneasy, *"closing"*, Reluctance, Tightness in shoulders.

TECHNIQUES FOR AMPLYFING INTUITIVE ABILITY

This first exercise is used in the corporate world due to its simplicity and effectiveness and because it takes less than 7 minutes. This exercise helps one more clearly connect with the feelings and sensations around the body which are responsible for how information is transmitted throughout the body.

1 - Practice Heart math for a few minutes by breathing in and out through your heart.

2 - Next imagine your attention and awareness moving to various regions around your body.

3 - Next become aware of how you feel at these various regions throughout your body. **ALLOW** yourself to feel changes in pressure, temperature and any tingling sensations you may feel.

4 - Become curious / inquisitive and explore what these sensations feel like.

If your attention ever wanders during this exercise, gently return your awareness to the sensations / feelings of various parts of your body.

5 - Next after you have fully **experienced the sensations**, thoughts and feelings, allow your awareness to EXPAND throughout your entire physical body.

6 - End the exercise.

INTUITIVE HEART TRUTHFULLNESS EXERCISE

Our heart always knows the truth and when we are not fully connected with it, it can alter the information or messages we receive when we seek intuitive information.

1 - Pay attention to how you feel around your heart

2 - Say out loud - "*Heart show me where you are now*"

3 - Next listen / feel for any sensations, colors etc. that flood your mind.

4 - Next breathe into these sensations while saying - *"Heart would you ever lie to me Yes or No?"*

5 – Next Ask – *"Heart will you always tell me the truth Yes or No?"*

6 - Thank your heart for its honesty and telling you the truth

BRAIN HEMISPHERE BALANCING EXERCISE

This exercise restores balance to both sides of the brain, which is a wonderful way to help enhance intuition.

1 - Place your left hand on the very back of your head.

2 - Place your right fingers directly on the top of your head.

3 - Next begin tapping the top of your head.

4 - After you have tapped the top of your head for a few moments, place your fingers in front of your heart and begin tapping your heart WHILE BREATHING IN and OUT.

5 - After a few exhales, move your left hand a few inches over the top of your head and begin tapping the top of your head again.

6 - Repeat again, while re-positioning your left hand upwards until it almost touches your forehead (a series of 3 to 4 cycles) then end and begin tapping the top of your head again.

You may have to re-position your tapping fingers as your left hand continues to move over the top of your head until it reaches your forehead. You can also practice this while standing up, turning from front to back (180 degrees) each time you re-position your hand on the top of your head.

THE RAISED ARM INTUITIVE METHOD

If you have to make a decision on the spot quickly, perform the following exercise -

1 - Hold both arms straight-out in front of you.

2 - Mentally affirm that your left arm represents the answer

"*yes*" and that your right arm represents the answer "*no*" or vice versa if you are left handed.

3 - Next mentally ask any question such as - "*Should I take on this new business venture?*" (or something similar that you feel uncertain about) .

4 - Next say out loud "*I ask the highest choice to please raise itself*".

5 - Next take a moment and pay attention to the feelings in your arms. The arm that wants to lift itself into the air will be the correct answer. When you receive the correct answer, you may also intuitively receive information about the question as well.

USING YOUR INTUITION TO MAKE THE RIGHT BUSINESS DECISION

1 - If you are attending an important business meeting, visualize in your mind the approximate time and place of the meeting before hand.

2 - Imagine the people who will be at the meeting.

3 - Breathe in and out 11 times - seeing love and light at the location the business meeting will be held.

4 – When the meeting takes place, and you are considering investing in the opportunity, use your intuition to sense the thoughts and feelings you feel from the people who are at the meeting.

BUSINESS MEETING INTUITIVE EXERCISE

If you are at an important meeting and you are uncertain about some of the individuals and their intention(s), perform the following exercise -

1 - Mentally reach out to individuals you are uncertain about and imagine your arm extending outwards, touching him or her in their heart.

2 - Next quiet your mind and allow your arm to quickly retract while asking the question "*How does this person feel? Excited,*

Angry, Edgy, Arrogant, Crooked, Safe, Loving, Kind etc."

or

*"How does this situation feel right now? Is this an honest
opportunity? Is the risk worth taking?"*

3 - The first feeling or emotions you receive before you can logically think about them will always be the right ones.

4 - Next ask the question - *"How do I feel?*

**All honest ideas that serve yourself and humanity
will be felt as positive energy that is
uplifting and will naturally carve
out their own road to success
without excessive struggle**

HOW TO TAKE RESPONSIBLE RISKS

Realizing the truth that fear is illusion is in itself an act of courage. **KNOW** that the universe **rewards** those who are bold and brave, for it is the law of the universe. The opportunity to profit from your divine gifts is unlimited due to the mere fact that nobody can do something as well as you can.

Just as all knowledge originates in the 5 senses, all change begins with a change in how we feel

The key to taking responsible risks and succeeding is knowledge and information. Preparing thoroughly and gathering enough information about what you want to invest in greatly reduces your chances of becoming involved in a risky deal. In any opportunity, it is wise to leave enough room for an exit strategy in case things go sideways and most importantly of all don't commit until you feel confident.

By learning to MONETIZE your gifts
and talents, you become
an inspiration
to others

CHAPTER 18
HOW TO LISTEN TO YOUR BODY'S SUBTLE MESSAGES TO ENJOY GOOD HEALTH

It is a now a scientific fact that excessive long term stress down regulates our genes, which causes chemical changes in the body which contribute to illness and dis-ease. This is because our cells were not meant to live in a stressful situation for extended periods of time. Hence, our environment influences our genes which create disease. Just by becoming more aware of something it reduces stress hormones and creates coherent brainwaves, which is why meditation can be used as a powerful healing tool.

The end product of experiences occurring in the environment cause emotions. Hence can our genes be signaled / controlled ahead of the environment by using positive / uplifting emotions? Research by Joe Dispenza discovered that participants (7,500 people) that took part in a meditation course for 4 days showed changes in 8 genes that lead to better health and a stronger immune system. So the answer is yes, changing genes through meditation can help one better cope with challenges in their environment.

A Harvard Study that was published in Psychological Science in 2007 found that a boring repetitive routine that was responsible for aches and pains was able to be transformed into something that is fun to do and in the process make one healthier. The study discovered that those who recognized their work as exercise experienced significant health benefits. The study involved approximately 100 room maids that worked in various hotels cleaning rooms. When they were instructed to think of the cleaning of their rooms as a form of outdoor exercise, they lost weight over a 4 week period, showed a reduction of body fat and exhibited lower blood pressure. All this just because they changed their **AWARENESS** of how they felt about what they did on a routine basis.

Reference

Mind-set matters: Exercise and the placebo effect. Crum, Alia J., and Ellen J. Langer. 2007. Psychological Science 18, no. 2: 165-171. 2007.

Making a wise decision to learn about something for sheer curiosity or fun, rather than just getting paid to learn is extremely valuable. This is because knowledge, skills and information are invaluable tools that can last a life-time.

This brings to mind the motion picture titled: **The Karate Kid**, where the instructor tells his student to paint the fence using an up / down motion. The student does this as instructed for days on end until it has become a boring routine. The teen sees this as being stupid because it has nothing to do with karate. Some weeks later, the instructor teaches the student how to block a deadly incoming punch. Because the student spent weeks painting the fence, his arm automatically raised itself with lightening sharp speed and blocked the deadly oncoming punch.

The same can be said for living in Hawaii. Many people here think that their jobs are boring and dull when abundance and health abounds. One could live their entire lifetime going on all the adventures, tours and expeditions and still not see everything the beautiful Hawaiian islands have to offer. Some people become frustrated and bored living here. However, diving instructors, artists, water sports enthusiasts or other activities that allow a person to **EXPERIENCE** and **FEEL** Hawaii, all enjoy living here. These people don't see their jobs as boring or routine, but instead as fun and exciting and share that happiness and excitement with the world.

WHY EDUCATED PEOPLE ENJOY BETTER OVERALL HEALTH

A fascinating research study that was published by Adesanya Oluwafunmilade and colleagues in November of 2017 titled: *Socioeconomic differential in self-assessment of health and happiness*, revealed that people who had no education or were less educated than average were at greater risk of experiencing poor health. It may be that the self-discipline necessary to study for and pass exams may enhance one's self-discipline when it comes to eating habits, physical activity and lifestyle.

HOW TO TURN YOUR BORING COMMUNTE INTO A SAFARI

The next time you drive to work, imagine yourself being on an adventure safari. Notice the sights, sounds and the small details in the environment along the way. Make each few hundred feet that goes by an adventure in itself. Notice things you didn't notice before, the sights, sounds and colors and experience it all through the eyes of a tourist taking in the journey for the very first time. Doing this simple technique only once will have you arrive at work in a much happier state of mind and you'll feel much better throughout the entire day. Get Creative!!!! Make an imaginary tour guide CD by adding sounds of elephants, tigers and birds. Narrate to yourself the highlights that exist along the road on your way to work, much like a tour guide speaks to tourists on a safari adventure.

CHAPTER 19
GOING BEYOND THE LAW OF ATTRACTION

Your inner being is naturally obeying the law of attraction by default; for better or for worse. Your mind has a natural focus to it that comes from who you believe yourself to be the most. Just like the law of gravity, the law of 

attraction dictates that you will eventually become what you believe.

The secret to a stronger attraction of anything is to share your happiness with others. When you share your happiness, you experience an expansion of it. This is why people who share their business in the forms of franchises, distributorships and affiliates succeed. For example, the founder of Kentucky Fried Chicken was so enthusiastic about his product that he spent a lot of time on the road selling his idea in person; even sleeping in his car some nights. Eventually his idea became popular worldwide..

BECOMING AWARE OF THE PROCESS OF CONSCIOUSNESS

Everything around us exists as pure energy; moving atoms vibrate so fast that we cannot see them and form the very book that you are reading right now. Learning to harness thoughts in order to control the energetic world we live in is key to manifesting desires and wants, as these vibrating atoms re-align themselves to manifest our desires. Because like attracts like, if you constantly worry or have thoughts of "*Oh there is never enough time, enough money, enough resources etc.*" your thoughts create a vibrational match which the universe recognizes. It will than set into motion events and circumstances that match that thought pattern. And because emotions amplify our feelings, which the universe responds to, the longer you dwell upon something, either good or bad, the more likely it will manifest. Meditation can help us see the forces of the law of attraction in real time because meditation puts us in touch with the reality that we are powerful beings with unlimited creative potential and that when we let go, resistance fades and we begin to experience who we truly are.

THE BEST LAW OF ATTRACTION TECHINQUES

- Make more of a conscious effort to become aware of the thoughts that stream through your mind on a daily basis; dismissing thoughts and ideas that are not aligned with your higher purpose.

- Set aside time to quiet the mind through meditation, which is remarkably effective at eliminating thoughts of fear, worry, doubt and anxiety.

A research study published in 2017 found that the number of people in the United States who practiced meditation tripled between 2012 and 2017, growing from 4.1% to 14.2%, with a similar increase in children practicing meditation (from 0.6% in 2012 to 5.4% in 2017).

Reference
Health Information. Meditation: In Depth. www.nccih.nih.gov.

Quote by the Dalai Lama - "*Violence and War would become extinct in 70 years or less, if at the beginning of age 5 children were taught to meditate on compassion for 60 minutes each week*".

Additional References
Changes in physician costs among high-cost Transcendental Meditation practitioners compared with high-cost non-practitioners over 5 years. Herron RE. Am J Health Promot. 2011;26:56–60.

Systematic review of the efficacy of meditation techniques as treatments for medical illness. Arias AJ, Steinberg K, Banga A, Trestman RL. J Altern Complement Med. 2006;12:817–32.

Stress, meditation, and Alzheimer's disease prevention: Where the evidence stands. Khalsa DS. J Alzheimers Dis. 2015;48:1–12.

The underlying anatomical correlates of long-term meditation: Larger hippocampal and frontal volumes of gray matter. Luders E, Toga AW, Lepore N, Gaser C. Neuroimage. 2009;45:672–8.

CHAPTER 20
THE ADVANTAGES OF HAVING HEALTHY SELF WORTH

Definition of Self-Worth - The Value you place upon your Soul

It is difficult to make a man miserable when he feels worthy of himself - Abraham Lincoln

Self worth, also known as self-love is a component of self-trust and self-esteem, all of which requires due diligence to maintain. Poor self worth originates from the false belief that life has never been there for you when you needed it most. This leads to thoughts such as -

"No one will ever be there to help me"

or

"I'm not deserving enough"

or

"I don't deserve it"

or

"Please feel sorry for me" and so on and so on ....

Self-worth is simply how well you treat yourself when under duress. This is because your soul can endure the hardest of hardships and why self-worth originates from the soul. Hence, every challenge life presents you with should be cherished because they are an opportunity for the soul to grow, when in turn adds strength to your overall feelings of self-worth.

Dupont Scientists discovered that atoms in the human body contain the potential power of 11 million kilowatt hours per pound of body weight. Hence, a person weighing 175-pounds could generate almost 2 billion kilowatt hours of power. Hence, the average man is worth about 85 million dollars (in electricity dollars).

Excessive self worth or self love leads to arrogance, excessive pride and feelings of inflated self-importance. It takes practice to express self love out of respect for what is worthy and right, without overbearing pride.

Poor self worth also allows one to fall victim to their circumstances. For example, some obese people know their self-destructive eating habits are the cause for their poor health condition. Hence, they allowed their poor self-worth to cause them to fall victim to their circumstances (*victim mentality*) and they eventually lost their self-control of eating healthy. The appearance of our physical body is a visible expression of the actions of the soul as it is shaped by our wants and desires. Just as one has to exercise their muscles in order for them to stay strong and healthy, one's inner self must also be exercised if positive change is to take place. Highly paid models who display the latest fashion clothing exude a strong presence of self-confidence and healthy self-worth. Feeling worthy is one of the few things you don't have to earn because self-worth comes from a place of "**what is**".

Theodore Roosevelt once said -
" *I do not care what others think about what I do, but I greatly care about what I think of what I do*"

Loving yourself is not conceit, rather it is a healthy conscious awareness of the ability to recognize that you have divine gifts and have been put on this planet to share them with the world. These gifts are to be honored, cherished and appreciated.

LEARNING TO VALUE THE SIMPLE
Our ego dismisses things that may seem small and insignificant to us, but hold great value. For example, when we pay for something, or work hard to achieve it, we give it much more

value than if we received it for free. Anything that is free, the ego finds hard to see the value in it. Things in life that are free such as appreciation, gratitude and healthy relationships are a few such examples.

KNOW that healthy self worth is not determined by your account balance, your living circumstances or the type of car you drive. A healthy sense of self worth is determined by how you treat yourself and how you see yourself; especially when under stress. It is normal to beat ourselves up at times in order to correct a mistake, however consistently beating oneself up results in low self-esteem over the long term. This is why self-worth is determined by the value you place upon your soul because the more you can endure a challenge without complaining about it, the brighter the light from your soul shines. KNOW you are worthy and deserving of all life wants to give you.

OUTWARD APPEARANCES CAN BE DECIEVING

If you were to get a brand new $100 note and have someone watch you place that $100 note in muddy wet soil and stomp on it until it has become saturated with dirt and mud and then asked the person "*Do you still want this $100?*" they will most likely say "*yes*". In summary, the $100 note has not lost any of its value.

Our sense of self-worth should not be based upon how well we perform something. This can be a trap for some professional athletes or for some who perform their profession in a public setting (*actors, singers etc*). In these settings, the person is identified by their great and exceptional talents, rather than for whatever self is behind the accomplishments (**his true self**). Hence, the person basis their self-worth on what they do, rather than who they truly are. This usually occurs in gifted people, mamy of whom are young. Hence, a false sense of self-worth comes from public achievements and the exaggerated approval from others. It is from this the person's identify is formed. Some salespeople are vulnerable to this, which is why good salespeople have learned to separate the results of their sales from how they perceive their sense of true self-worth.

When a person bases their entire self-worth based solely upon their performance, when that person fails, which is inevitable, the person takes the failure very personal, with self-worth plummeting in the process. This can lead to a negative self-image. The antidote to this is to **INSTILL** a **NEW SET** of ideals and values that will build self-worth based upon who they truly are. One can do this by learning the following -

- ➤ If you are into sports, learn to develop a more aggressive style

- ➤ Become more focused

- ➤ Take steps to become more well rounded; valuing more in life. Volunteering is one example

- ➤ Learn to **EVALUATE** your actions and efforts in your work or profession

- ➤ Set standards based upon values, and become accountable by evaluating your actions

- ➤ Learn to take responsibility, rather than blame. Know that the consequences for something you do is not going to mean the end of the world.

- ➤ View life objectively

- ➤ Tolerate uncertainly when necessary

- ➤ Identify inner defense mechanisms that you erect in life and work on breaking them down. By doing this, you eventually learn to realize that you no longer need to continually justify yourself to others.

> Learn to build a strong sense of your esteemed self, which involves courage, intelligence and how you approach challenges.

Most of all understand that healthy self-worth is related to your substance (**who you are**) rather than what you do (or are praised for). It is a fact that academic potential has absolutely nothing to do with your potential for self-life mastery. The Wright Brothers who invented the first working airplane never graduated high school; neither did the richest man in the world Bill Gates graduate college. These people had faith and believed in their product and that they would ultimately succeed; and they did.... You are a divine creation which originated in the world of Spirit and have all the skills you need to accomplish all you came here to do. One must learn to develop and identify the difference between self-worth and how one views their accomplishments and learn to develop the substance of who they really are; **his substantial self**.

Quote by Lucretius - "*Look at the man in the midst of doubt and danger, mask torn off, yet danger remains*"

We are fortunate as human beings in that our soul has the power to differentiate limitlessly from the Infinite. Our soul is a direct reflection of Infinite Spirit. It shows us that it cannot be anything else and that our mere **RECOGNITION** of this power is the whole force that is responsible for the creative process. If our souls did not possess an unlimited power of differentiation from the Infinite, than the Infinite would not be able to be reflected in it. Consequently

Wise Words of Wisdom

—

The accomplishment of a desire will fail to materialize if one allows the expectations of others to become their sole objective in life

Source would have no outlet and NOT BE ABLE to express Life, Love, and Beauty.

YOUR DIVINE GIFTS ARE MEANT TO BE USED

We all use our divine gifts to some degree within our lives. Some people use them more than others. One example that really helps bring this home is to imagine yourself, old and gray and on your death bed. As the dimly lit room gets dark from the sun falling in the sky, you see a series of small oval-shaped figures that you can barely make out in the dim light. As they approach you, you see they represent the divine gifts and talents that the universe gave to you. As you make eye contact with these figures they scream out " *Why did you ignore us? We were given to you by God. How come you failed to use us? We feel let   down!!!!"*

Learning to use our divine gifts to manifest and attract to us what we want pleases the invisible forces watching over us because we had to learn LIFE lessons in order to acquire them.

How many people today maximize and make use of their God given gifts and talents to their utmost potential? We have been given an opportunity and a responsibility to make use of these gifts. Our physical form is a manifestation of Divine Energy which our soul experiences as a temporary existence in a physical body. As we grow older and become more included to adhere to con-formality we lose touch with this important link to the Divine. To re-establish this link, say to yourself -

"The divine is a multifaceted rainbow with each spark of life representing each raindrop. I exist as but one of these raindrops; therefore thoughts of lack, scarcity or limitation are inherently foreign to me."

Because you are made from the divine, and contain within you a part of it, it is impossible to think such thoughts as -

"I am too mean a person ever to reflect so glorious an image"

or

"God never intended such a limitless ideal to be reproduced in human beings."

Ask yourself, *"If nobody ever told me who I was, who would I be?*

SUMMARY
It is the order of nature itself not to be unworthy because it exists as a piece of Divine creation and it is not possible for a Divine creation to experience feelings of unworthiness.

ADVANCED TECHNIQUES FOR DEVELOPING SELF-WORTH
One secret to rapidly experience self-love or self worth is to be conscious of the thoughts you think.

1 - Write down a description of the person you would like to become.

2 - Next follow through by acting the part of the successful person you want to become.

3 - Ask yourself - "*What would the millionaire version of me do?*'

LEARNING TO ACCEPT COMPLIMENTS
Gratitude is the ultimate state of receiving because when you receive something, you are giving thanks and are grateful for receiving   it.
    Learning to accept compliments puts you in receiving mode. To begin with, allow yourself to experience the uncomfortable feeling of receiving compliments until you feel comfortable   receiving   them.
    Gratitude is the ultimate state of receiving because when you receive something you are giving thanks and are grateful for receiving   it.

Another trick, which requires a little more self-discipline is to eat nutritious food, especially when your body is requesting it. What better way to be good to your body and the planet at the same time by becoming vegetarian?

DIVINE ENTITLEMENT

Allowing yourself to feel divinely entitled to abundance for the right reasons gives one the confidence because one **KNOWS** they are worthy of profiting from their divine skills and talents. If you have ever watched the movie **Coming to America** by Eddie Murphy, he portrays the role of a wealthy Royal African Prince that comes to the United States to find a wife. The movie is an excellent example of what it truly feels like to experience worthiness. The prince is not boastful, bragging or harsh. Instead his attitude is one of deserving and feeling worthy. This is an excellent movie for anyone wanting to incorporate a self-deserving mindset.

A life of Discovery

If a youngster left school at 10 years of age, with the bare necessities of knowing how to read and write, but knowing nothing of the details of information; yet he knew the pure pleasure that comes from music that is uplifting and moves the soul or from making things and finding things out himself; he would grow up better off than someone who left university at 22 with a mind filled with facts, but devoid of any desire to inquire further into such dry domains.

Great men succeeded by following their curiosity in a subject and though experimentation or mentors eventually hit on the correct approach.

CHAPTER 21
EXPERIENCING CONTENTment FOR EFFORTLESS WEALTH AND ABUNDANCE

Real lasting long term financial abundance comes from learning to cultivate happiness from within. This creates **FEELINGS** of **CONTENTMENT**, which helps you recognize the existing abundance that is already around you. Being ready to receive is not enough, one must first learn to be happy on the inside first, then what one desires the most will manifest.

There are 2 types of people who are primarily un-happy in life when they think about money -

1 - The Ultra Rich
2 - The Ultra Poor

The reason for this is because both groups of people are always thinking about money; either by thinking they don't have enough or fears of losing it all.

PRACTICING EFT FOR EXPERIENCING HAPPINESS

A study involving participants enrolled in a 4-day workshop that practiced the EFT technique, showed significant declines in anxiety (-40%), depression (-35%), posttraumatic stress disorder (-32%), pain (-57%), and cravings. The study also found that Happiness increased (+31%, P = .000) and that the participants exhibited beneficial health benefits including HRV.

PRACTICING SMILING INTO YOUR HEART FOR CONTENTMENT

One effective method to cultivate inner happiness from within is to practice the **Inner Smile Technique**.

1- Connect with your heart by imagining your awareness around your heart area

2 - Next simply imagine yourself smiling into your heart Because the universe operates on the principle of feelings, the more content we feel, the more we attract. This re-affirms the saying quoted in one of the most popular books of all time -

"Whoever has will be given more, and he will have an abundance. Whoever does not have, even what he has will be taken away from him." Matthew 25:29

When you learn to KNOW that you already live in a state of abundance, feelings of contentment allow your lifestyle of wealth to manifest much more rapidly. Aligning one's thoughts with ACTION removes fear, doubt and worry by creating PURPOSE from which authentic power is derived because your personality is now aligned with the purpose of your soul.

By exercising spiritual & emotional strength at the right moments, you will discover that it leads to feelings of contentment.

TIPS FOR EXPERIENCING CONTETMENT

Being able to meet your needs and pay your bills creates feelings of contentment. This re-affirms to your subconscious that you are already wealthy. Learn to generate sustained happiness from within as well as feel gratitude. Imagine yourself already living in a joyous environment that is comfortable, has easy access to everything you need and exists in a loving, caring community. These 2 simple acts fuel the glowing embers of contentment. The satisfaction of having successfully conquered a challenge also creates feelings of contentment and satisfaction. Below is a simple contentment exercise.

1 - Two or three times a day connect with the inner happiness that already exists within you.

2 - Next align these feelings of happiness with your heart.

3 - Next allow your heart to recognize this.

4 - Next merge your feelings of happiness with your heart, seeing it merge into a single form of energy.

5 - Experience how you **now feel different**, knowing you are experiencing true contentment.

Additional tips for generating contentment -
Have gratitude for the essentials in your life such as the abundance of air, sunshine, water, the warmth of a fire, nature's animals and all other creatures that make up the abundant world.

- Create a space within that mirrors feelings of joy and peace; an inner island or sanctuary of contentment.

- Volunteer at a worthy cause.

- Tithing. This is giving back 10% of what you earn to a worthy organization that supports someone in need.

- Share your happiness and excitement with others.

- RECOGNIZE that what currently exists in your life is enough, all that you have is plenty and all your needs are being met.

- RECOGNIZE the feelings you have within you such as peace, satisfaction and fulfillment.

- ALLOW yourself to **EXPERIENCE** feelings of contentment.

The saying is true, the best things in life are not just free, but also the most simplistic.

As above, so below, *AS WITHIN, SO WITHOUT*

CHAPTER 22
INTIMIDATION = LIMITATION

An MIT study found that if somebody views someone as an authority figure and that authority figure says to them - *"You can't do this!"* or *"You can't do that"* or *"You're no good!"* that if the person that received the negative remark wants to neutralize it, they only have to repeat 17 times the phrase *"you can do it!!"* or *"I can do this"* with power, feeling and conviction.

Reference
Beyond the Secret. Les Brown

Those lacking ambition are more likely to intimidate other people and if one submits to intimidation it can reinforce one's limiting beliefs. We become intimated by feeling powerless due to circumstances we feel are beyond our control. However we do have power over how we RESPOND to our circumstances. KNOW that the divine light of wisdom IS truth and that **TRUTH** is the **ULTIMATE AUTHORITY**. Learn to REJECT any form of authority that does not radiate truth or forces its own agenda unfairly upon you.

Wise Words of Wisdom Regarding Truth

- The nature of truth is that all it asks and wants is the liberty of making its presence known. Hence truth does not seek to rule us or exert an agenda of its own.

- Those who distort the truth live uncomfortable lives because truth cannot be distorted or made into someone else's version of it.

- Truth cannot be fully realized until it has permeated the very substance of our life by good habits.

Discover for yourself the truth about who you really are (abundant, radiant, powerful, creative, possessed of unlimited potential, abundance is your birthright). **RECOGNIZE** your divine gifts and talents and that they hold **VALUE**, than express them to the world.

CHAPTER 23
REMOVING BLOCKS AND LIMITATIONS ABOUT MONEY

You wouldn't have picked up this book if you did not have some type of money block. Everyone has money blocks to some degree. Perhaps you were deprived of something, or you were told that you would never be able to accomplish anything you desired. For some of you reading this, you may have already tried removing money blocks, but became frustrated because you discovered that they didn't work. Money blocks block us from experiencing "*Abundance Consciousness*" also called "*Prosperity Consciousness*". It is the state of mind where we are aware of the infinite order of things.

WHAT ARE MONEY BLOCKS?

Money blocks are the result of energy blockages coming from previous beliefs or beliefs that are outdated or don't support one's ambitions. Many blocks come from early childhood experiences that we believed to be true.

A person with a healthy financial life has a firm and clear blueprint of their future financial goals. This causes the person to experience a healthy and expanding circulating flow of radiant wealth, allowing them to give and receive simultaneously. Some people experience rapid healings after their money blocks have been removed because they have gotten in touch with their true feelings. **Energetic Architecture Clearings** are one method that have been successfully used to erase money blocks because the process restores order and balance to one's energetic field. However, Energetic Clearings are just a part of the overall process of removing money blocks and should not be relied upon entirely if one seeks solid and consistent financial growth.

KNOW that the universe has no limits, is free of lack or limitation and is constantly expanding. Hence, a belief mindset that supports your abundance mindset allows you to manifest more clearly and rapidly because it is properly aligned with the law of **EXPANSION**. Money blocks can also be an excuse to sustain the ego in order to enforce its version of how reality should play out; causing controlling behaviors. This further moves one's energetic blueprint from one of order and harmony to one of chaos and imbalance. Over time the person becomes disconnected from their inner self, which results in a loss of their ability to be guided by their Higher Self.

When one's energetic architectural blueprint has been restored, one experiences an energetic balance because homeostatic functioning in Mind, Body, Soul and Spirit have been restored. One now knows who they truly are;   a multidimensional being and the person enthusiastically experiences exhilaration and enthusiasm for life.

HOW DO I KNOW IF REMOVING A MONEY BLOCK HAS ACTUALLY WORKED?

Look at your circumstances; they will be a direct reflection of your current beliefs about money. Hence if you have not found, exposed or got to the CORE ROOT of a lack of financial abundance, you will still be experiencing blockages, which causes one to become *stuck*. If you find that you have done all the exercises and still have money blocks, than Energetic Clearings by an experienced practitioner are really the only final solution.

Beliefs learned early in life stick around for an entire lifetime, especially if we live in an environment that does not challenge us. Unexpected challenges take us on new journeys because they involve risks most people are unwilling to take.

After money blocks have been cleared, there is usually a short-term temporary increase in income which usually manifests within 24 to 72 hours or less. You may have already seen numerous websites promoting this because it works. However, one should not become overconfident at this, because if you think your money blocks are gone, they are not.

HOW HABITUAL THINKING CREATES YOUR REALITY

For some people their current belief system creates the following repetitive thoughts -

Life is hard. I have to work hard. Struggle, pain and challenge are the normal lot in life. I never have enough. Scarcity is everywhere.

**Law of the Universe - You <u>BECOME</u> what *you*
BELIEVE you are the most**

ENERGETIC CLEARINGS FOR REMOVING MONEY BLOCKS

One prevailing false belief in our society is that you have to work hard all the time to make money. Nothing could be further from the truth. Just look at all the wealthy people who have acquired enough assets so that their money works for them. Energetic blockages usually begin small, than build up over time, eventually manifesting as feelings of restriction or resistance.

HOW ENERGETIC CLEARINGS WORK

All objects, buildings and other solid forms in our reality first began in the mind as an energetic blueprint, similar to a blueprint for a building. This blueprint was based upon a specific set of beliefs at the time the blueprint was drawn. This is why modern buildings look so much different than historical buildings. The secret about using Energetic Clearings is to be as detail specific as possible about what you want (*dollar amount, what you are willing to do, and other details*) combined with a clear focused intention. This then allows the universe to fill in the remaining gaps. Then all you need do is let go, relax and allow yourself to be open to receive.

An Energetic Clearing locates patterns of dis-chord and disharmony occurring in the mental emotional part of a person's body. The person's limited beliefs create feelings and emotions which restrict the flow of energy in their emotional body.

Energetic Architecture Clearings locate specific patterns of dis-chord occurring in a financial blueprint. This disorder comes from a limited belief mindset which generates feelings and corresponding emotions that cause restriction.

When one experiences an energetic clearing, one does so in an expanded state of mind where the old patterns become Energetically Deleted. **Expansion = Order**. Because your desire now exists more clearly in Spirit, you just need to take action to see your goals realized. Energetic Architecture Clearings need to be practiced whenever you feel money flow is beginning to become constricted. These blocks usually begin showing up as your profits or income begin growing.

Some Energetic Clearing Exercises use white light. This is because each and every one of us intuitively knows about "**the light**". We experience it when we pray, when we contemplate, when we visualize a ring of protection and when we feel really, really good. Our soul is naturally drawn to the light, wanting to feel nourished by it because it generates feelings of satisfaction and peace.

STUDIES SHOW THAT THINKING OF WHITE LIGHT ALTERS BRAIN CHEMISTRY

Studies have found that participants visualizing white light exhibited profound increases in the biophoton counts emitted from the right side of their head. Increases in the power emitted within the parahippocampal region of the participant's brains was observed with frequencies in the region between 6 Hz and 17 Hz. This frequency range is also in the same frequency range as earth's Schuman Resonance, which is a standing wave resonance taking place in earth's Ionosphere. The Schuman Resonance is caused by lightening striking the ground. What is interesting about this frequency range is that it falls within the range of 10hz, which is a frequency that naturally reduces anxiety in the body.

Reference
The Impact of Monaural Beat Stimulation on Anxiety and Cognition. Leila Chaieb et al. May 2017.

In 4 independent research studies the researchers observed increases in biophoton emissions from the right side of the participant's head (with almost zero increases observed on the left). These significant increases occurred when the participants merely thought about white light *(Hunter et al 2010; Dotta & Persinger 2011; Dotta et al 2012; Saroka et al 2013)*. The research conducted by Dotta and colleagues in 2012 observed that the increase in biophoton emissions was able to be measured from the right hemisphere of participants who visualized white light *(Dotta et al 2012)*.

THE SUPERIMPOSITION TRANSFER OF INFORMATION
In other experiments one group of participants was exposed to magnetic fields. Once this occurred, the other participant registered an increase in their biophoton count *(Biophoton Detection and Low-Intensity Light Therapy: A Potential Clinical Partnership Joseph Tafur, et al. Feb 2010)*.

SUMMARY
Because our brain's left side performs tasks that result in logic type functions such as mathematics and science and the right hemisphere performs tasks involving creativity, intuition and the arts, it may be that just by merely thinking about white light that it helps one more clearly connect with their intuition, creativity and artistic talents.

WHAT ARE BIOPHOTONS?
Biophotons are tiny particles of barely visible light (*including UV light*) that are found in various concentrations around the body, most notably the finger tips and head regions of the body. Biophoton technology is a newly emerging science and is being explored for the early detection of many types of diseases. In simple terms, the healthier the biophotons in your body, the

healthier your body is. The best part about biophotonic technology is that it is non-invasive, making early detection of diseases painless. There exist numerous research studies about biophotonic healing and the science of this is out of the scope of this book. It is my belief that the thinking about white light helps one more fully realize their connection to their subconscious mind.

Energetic Architecture Clearings are not only able to get to the CORE reason a money block exists, but CREATE a new future financial blueprint that re-shapes one's current beliefs about money. When we imagine what we want, a blueprint takes shape on the higher Spiritual planes and this blueprint can be greatly energized just by simply visualizing pure white light. What is very interesting is that Architects place blueprints over a box filled with white light to make the blue prints more easy to read. What a great way to show the connection between a Spiritual Blueprint and Construction Blueprints.

One common question is "*How do I know if I have money blocks after an energetic clearing, belief re-programming exercise or other self-help method?*" The answer is to look at your current circumstances. These will be a direct reflection of your current beliefs about money. Hence, over time if money blocks still keep occurring, than you have not found the CORE ROOT of a money block. Another method is to look up an experienced Energetic Architecture Clearing practitioner to help remove money blocks.

Further Reading

Detecting presence of cardiovascular disease through mitochondria respiration as depicted through biophotonic emission. Nancy R.Rizzo et al. October 2010.

CHAPTER 24
RECONNECTING WITH FLOW

We experience impulses that guide us towards our goals as subtle urges occurring in the flow of life which consists of feelings of joy and abundance. To experience flow is to be free of resistance. Getting in flow affords one the ability to re-experience being alive and aware. When you are "*in flow*" there is no resistance; you naturally feel good. Your desires are aligned with the Divine. Experiencing flow allows one to become fluid and fast on their feet, preparing for the unexpected. This is why luck is seen as flow, because all luck really is, is preparing ahead of time for opportunity.

To experience Flow, put Desire into Motion by having faith in the final outcome

One can get back into the flow of synchronicity by allowing one to re-connect with the flow. Emotions such as Love, Eagerness and Happiness all re-connect one back to flow.

Tips to get in touch with Flow -

- Laughter
- Moderate exercise that challenges you physically
- Experiencing Nature
- Find something you appreciate and allow gratitude to fill your heart. Love, Gratitude, Kindness, Forgiveness all instantly reconnect you back to flow.

Spiritual practices can also help one connect more easily with flow. Examples include -

- o Seeing the God in people

- o Having the Courage to Love

- o Expect the best

- o Seeing the best in everyone

- o Doing good deeds

CAN BAD LUCK BE CHANGED?

There is no such thing as luck; either good or bad. There is however ignorance and a lack of forethought and careful planning. Money is seen as good luck because the wealthy have the necessary resources to plan ahead and avoid misfortune by investing in resources that create lasting peace of mind. On the other hand, the opposite is also true. Criminals who steal do so because they see in money the good fortune that they lack in their lives.

6 SIMPLE STEPS TO ENHANCE THE GOOD LUCK IN YOUR LIFE

1 - Prepare for opportunities you deem valuable well ahead of time.

2 - Follow your purpose in life. Nothing stands in the way of a well-defined purpose.

3 - Be courageous. Backing down breeds stagnation.

4 - Practice Kindness and Courtesy. You may need to call upon your reservoir of kind acts in the future when you least expect it.

5 - Burn some incense.

6 – If you fail at something, see the remaining possibilities that exist.

7 – Use the appropriate opportunities in your exit strategy when planning to take risks.

Affirmation - ***Divine Spirit paves my way to make this day***

KNOW that problems are not problems unless you give them your constant attention. Learn to detach part of your thinking from the little things that worry you because the little things eventually work themselves out along the way.   Hence the saying   *"Don't   sweat   the   small   stuff!!!."*

THE LAW OF KARMA

Karma, or the thoughts, words, deeds and actions we express on a daily basis determine how we will experience the future. Energy that you put out to help and assist others **ALWAYS** returns to you in greater measure.   The opposite is also true; energy that you misuse and harm others with will decrease the abundance and prosperity in your life. **This is universal law.**

A TECHNIQUE FOR MANIFESTING GOOD LUCK

1 - Get a piece of paper and write out 10 things that matter to you the most.

2 - Next label the things you wrote down on paper that are troubling you or things that may not be going as good as you want them to be.

3 - Now spend effort focusing on the things that are currently going well for you, even if it is just one small thing. You will soon find that the things that are not going well will start turning around, just by focusing on the things that are going well. This comes from the old saying - ***"A rising tide lifts all boats."***

A TECHNIQUE FOR STARTING OUT YOUR DAY ON THE RIGHT FOOT

Sometimes our days may seem mundane, boring and repetitious, which can evoke feelings of frustration and discontent. This can be solved by understanding that we live in a world dominated by frequency and the repetitive acts we perform each day create the dominant frequency that we experience in our day-to-day lives.

Oscillation creates frequency. An example of oscillation is the number of times it takes for the end of a pendulum to swing from left to right within a certain amount of time. Hence a new oscillation can simply be created by creating a new habitual routine. So the next time you get up in the morning, make a firm commitment to create a new oscillation in your environment. You may only need to make this commitment once or twice each morning and not need to do it again for the rest of the week or even month, but you will find that when you go out to start your day, that things will go much smoother.

Recognize Your Value

The same **RECOGNITION** of the abundance that already exists around you, learn to **RECOGNIZE** the value in your divine gifts when you offer or utilize them and allow the world to RECOGNIZE and reward you for the **VALUE** they contain. Know that you are worthy and deserving of receiving **MONETARY COMPENSATION** for your divine skills gifts and talents. Combine this with the deservingness that you deserve to be divinely compensated for your divine skills, gifts and talents, than abundance will flow to you naturally......

Chapter 25
RAISING YOUR STANDARDS AVOIDS STAGNATION

Whatever you perform the most on a daily basis and have become good at is the standard that you have set for yourself. What we want in our lives is not often achieved because of the standards we have set. For example, for some people their outward physical appearance is based upon their standards. Hence, a sports athlete has different standards compared to a non-professional athlete. This is because the standards of a professional athlete have become a **NEED**, which must be consistently met. Because most of us go through our daily lives on autopilot, standards that we set for ourselves 10 or even 20 years ago may still be playing out in our lives. When we forget to upgrade our standards when we set out to achieve our goals or desires, our ego will trick us into returning to what is safe and familiar.

True strength does not come from physical exercise, it comes from an indomitable will

FAMILARITY AND THE INEVEITABILITY OF CHANGE
The familiar feels good because we have been conditioned by our ego to think so. It becomes a natural habit to retreat from change. However the will to make major changes is sometimes put into motion when circumstances occur that are beyond our control. Familiarity ends and the ego temporarily fades into the distance, like a distant sunset.

Remaining in the comfort zone, especially if your financial goals have not been met breeds stagnation. Excess comfort may reduce the quality of service and value you are offering, restricting growth. KNOW that growth requires some sacrifices. KNOW that as changes take place when you move out of your comfort zone, that the pain of regret by giving up is far deeper than the temporary discomfort experienced as you pursue your goals.

NATURE'S ROLE OF REMOVING STAGNATION

The seasons, our life circumstances, including our emotions are all in a constant state of change. This is due to the law of rhythm. Nature is fearless. The forces of wind and rushing water are constantly flowing about, washing away stagnation, making way for the new. Because fear, worry and doubt contribute to stagnation, initiating action removes these stagnant emotions. Thoughts of one thinking they are perfect and that they don't need to change breeds stagnation which results primarily from ignorance, caused by the ego.

SIMPLE TECHNIQUES THAT RAISE YOUR STANDARDS

You hold within you the power to shape your outside environment though sheer mental will. Find something that will give you fulfillment and satisfaction when deciding to raise your standards. Break down your largest daily or weekly objectives into small bite size chunks, celebrating your small victories along the way. RECOGNIZING your small victories will help keep you motivated.

SUMMARY

Setting higher standards and adhering to them requires self-discipline; however know that the minor insolvencies you encounter at first when adhering to your higher standards is far less bitter than the pain of regret should you unexpectedly give up.

Chapter 26
LEVERAGING OUT YOUR EFFORTS

Leverage is a tool that multiplies your efforts. For example if you invented a widget and sold it one widget at a time from business to business the amount of sales you make is determined by how many hours there are in each day (the time you have). However, if you started a distributorship, having people selling the widget for you, you reach more people in less time; hence you have the ability to make more profit because you have leveraged your efforts.

By investing in the latest technology, reading the latest books by experts and exploring new ways of marketing and networking your product or service, you can discover tried and proven strategies that will uncover new ways of creating leverage to sell your service or product. Another key is to have a good mentor that can teach you invaluable lessons about how him or her leverages their time.

Other methods of leverage include -
- Affiliate market your product or service
- Expanded networking

LEARNING TO LEVERAGE INTENTION

There is a way to leverage your intention by using the law of expansion. Simply align your heart with your stated intention or goal with your feelings. This simple technique results in your goal manifesting in far better ways than you could have imagined. When you include using your heart to bring expansion to your intentions you will soon discover that what you envisioned manifests in far greater measure. Some people may fear aligning their heart with their intention because they fear losing their individuality or working on the inner plane (*the inner plane being our thoughts, beliefs and actions*). However, the only way the outer world ever changes is when changes are made in the inner world. Also it is important to remember that just like muscles need to be exercised in order to remain strong, over time as one learns to exercise their inner muscles, they discover that changes in the outer world occur in direct proportion to the amount of effort put forth in the inner world.

It is the nature of heart energy to expand, and as it expands, its energy paves over hidden obstacles taking care of all of the little details. One learns that this expansive energy is magnetic and as it expands, it draws the outer world of material desire to onc like a magnet though synchronicity. Know that it makes complete sense that the universe is loving, supportive and abundant; that your **abundance is already there waiting for you** to claim it. All you need do is show up and participate.

HOW TO LEVERAGE AN AFFIRMATION

First state your affirmation than recognize the source that is supporting you Spiritually. For example -

I have faith in myself by having faith in the universe

I am worthy and deserving and the universe is worthy and deserving of my participating in it.

I am grateful for my monthly income now becoming my weekly income

I am grateful for my yearly income now being my monthly income

I am unconditionally blessed and blessed unconditionally

I am so happy and grateful for having the opportunity to express feelings of gratitude

LEVERAGING THE POWER OF EXPECTATION

Because we are constantly co-creating our future with the ultimate creator, what better way to effortlessly manifest success than to expect that the best is yet to come. Expect the best.

Use your bills to empower your powers of expectation. If the person you pay your bills to on a regular basis sees that you are requesting an upgrade or applying for a premium service, it affirms to the universe that you are doing well. For example, if you pay for something on a regular basis, instead of paying the regular amount, pay double for what you currently pay for. If you visit your local health supplement store every few weeks and you usually purchase the small sized economy pack of multivitamins, next time purchase the large size and silently affirm to yourself that you are doing twice as well financially. This will affirm to the universe that you are doing well financially.

Another example is if you go to the gym, and the gym offers upgrades such as a premium membership, purchase this add-on, even if it is for just a couple of months.

FAKE IT TILL YOU MAKE IT

Creating an outward appearance of success is one excellent way to attract positive opportunity and express your personal power. Expect the best - Walk, talk and act like you have already achieved what you desire and opportunity and showers of blessings will come your way. Know that the Universe always delivers when you exercise trust and faith in it.

CHAPTER 27
TECHNIQUES FOR CONNECTING WITH THE GOD WITHIN

How close you are to connecting to the God Within is how in flow you are with life. When you are not at ease with yourself, it is a hint that a new direction in your life is starting to carve itself out. There is a supreme moment of destiny for all of us. It is our job to listen to that.

ACTIVATING THE GOD WITHIN EXERCISE

When one visualizes a god and at the same time tunes into the God within and imagines the God within also tuning into the desired goal, it creates a powerful creative synergy. Learning to connect to the God within is one of the most simple and most effective methods to seek advice, guidance or wisdom in a hurry.

1 - Tune into the God within

2 - See the God within **RECOGNIZING** your goal

3 - Align your goal with the God within, becoming ONE

4- After seeing them both as ONE hold the vision in your mind and fill your goal with joyful play and spontaneous energy. Hold this in your mind only as long as you feel comfortable.

4 - Allow and accept any new feelings that emerge; you will notice new sensations in your body. This is healthy and normal.

5 - Detach, let go, allowing the vision to manifest itself in its own good time

ASK THE GOD WITHIN TO -

- Reveal sound investment advice and opportunities

- Reveal to you sound investment advisors and or money managers

- Reveal to you your divine skills, gifts, talents and abilities

- Reveal your true calling in life

Ask the following if you want to seek advice from the God within -

Ask the God within - *"Tell me what to do about this?"*

or

"I ask the God within to guide and direct me towards ...."

or

"I ask the God within for wisdom in this matter" or *"I ask the God within to help me solve this problem"*

or

"God within me, show me how to prosper and in the process, bless myself and others"

or

"I ask the God within to give me prospering ideas"

or

"I ask the God within to reveal my gifts, talents and abilities".

Spontaneous Activity, Excitement, Celebration, Passion and Enthusiasm all align you with the Divine

"I Petition the God within_______________________"

CHAPTER 28
THE BEST MIND POWER TECHNIQUES THAT ELIMINATE DISTRACTION

PROTECTING WHAT IS VALUABLE TO YOU

Have you ever tried to grow a fruit tree or vegetables in a home garden? If you don't protect the young plants, they will be attacked by pests. When you nurture and protect the young plants they yield forth their bounty of plenty. The same is with our goals or objectives. When we first set out to achieve them, we may experience attacks, especially as we near the completion of our goal or objective.

A TECHNIQUE THAT RIDS BOTHERSOME PEOPLE #1 -

1 - If you find that someone is constantly bothering you and won't go away, as you start your day, mentally blow out love and light ahead of you as you get up in the morning. Or recite the phrase – *"Divine **spirit paves my way to make this day"***

2 - Next sit quietly and relax and see the person bothering you in your mind's eye.

3 - Mentally bring them up close to you, eyeball to eyeball and breathe in.

4 - As you expel your breath, breathe out into their heart, sending them love and light.

The first few minutes upon waking, the mind does not consciously experience fear

5 - Do this 11 times in a row or for a minimum of 17 minutes. This will cause an energetic shift to take place between you and the person. If you still see the person, the next time you see them, they will respond differently to you.

BOTHERSOME PEOPLE REMOVAL TECHNIQUE #2 -

IF YOU WISH TO SEE SOMEONE REMOVED FROM YOUR LIFE

1 - After doing step 4 in the above exercise, visualize the person in the palm of your hand being small and tiny.

2 - Look down upon them from above, seeing them standing in the palm of your hand, about 1 inch in height.

3- Next move your hand up to your mouth and expel a short sharp breath at the small person.

4 - Literally see them being blown away with your sharp breath, while repeating 3 times - *"I release you with love and light. Go in peace to your highest good, but GO!!!!"*

5 - Perform this technique for a minimum of 4 days in a row for maximum effect. Some people have reported that using this technique causes a person's negative energy to be deflected back to them, causing him or her to become mentally confused or overstressed,

A TECHNIQUE TO GET RID OF BOTHERSOME PEOPLE #3 -

1 - Write down on a piece of paper 10 things you are grateful for in your life. Do this every morning for 5 days in a row.

2 - Next mentally project pure unconditional love to 3 people that are bothering you. Send this love by prayer or by focused mental intent.

3 - Next share this technique with somebody. Either in person, mentally or online.

If you like, you can share the technique with close friends or family, having members write down on a piece of paper 10 things they are currently grateful for every morning.

CHAPTER 29
TECHNIQUES AND EXERCISES FOR CULTIVATING WEALTH CONSCIOUSNESS

Technique #1 - Carry around with you a $100 note (or up to $300 in $100 notes) in your wallet just for a day or so and notice how people respond to you differently. The response comes from how you feel because you are exhibiting more confidence.

FANCY FACT - The life expectancy of U.S. coins are approximately 30 years. Small notes last approximately 2 years and $100 bills last approximately 10 years.

You cannot out give God

Technique #2 - When you take money to deposit into your bank account, take 2 deposit slips, 1 with a deposit for 1 million dollars (*which is make believe*) and the other one for your usual deposit. Keep your 1 million dollar deposit slip with you and put it where you see it most often.

Technique #3 - Carry a spare $20 note in your wallet and when you see someone that is trying to make a positive impact on the world, or that you feel is genuinely in need give it to them. Giving back generates perceived abundance, even if it exists for just one brief moment.

Wise Words of Wisdom – Gratitude is the sole process of absolute mental adjustment

CHAPTER 30
AFFORMATIONS FOR WEALTH AND PROSPERITY

Affirmations empower your soul allowing you to experience true authentic power as you express your personality.

When saying any of the affirmations listed below, say the affirmation with **MEANING**. Other times you may need to say the words with faith and conviction and at other times with sincerity and intent. Over time as the phrases are repeated they will grow in power, creating new habits. In most instances after repeating an affirmation, you may feel impulses that will tend to guide you in the right direction. Follow them, no matter how subtle, as they are guiding you to your goal or objective. Read a few of these each day after writing in your gratitude journal to create a firm foundational mindset of prosperity and abundance that   will   last   throughout   your   day.

Affirm   the   following   affirmations   like   they   are   an established fact. You can also add power to your affirmations by writing them down on paper. As you read the words, mentally rehearse you having already received what you are seeking. See the positive impact that the money will have upon your life and those you choose to invest money in such as charities, investing in new ideas etc. Create a mental movie with emotions as if it has already happened. **Write - Feel - Visualize**. Feel free **to** photocopy the following affirmations on the next few pages and stick them around your home or car where you will see them throughout the day.

Write out - "*I see myself receiving \$_______ immediately to enable me to___________*".

- *I affirm my wealth and abundance and am grateful for the riches that are now freely accessible to me.*

- *I have plenty to give and I love to share.*

- *When I pay for something, I visualize the same notes (only larger) returning to my bank account and wallet.*

- *I am financially wealthy and spiritually wealthy.*

- *I gratefully accept all the wealth and abundance from the universe that flows into my life every day.*

- *I affirm that I receive treasures and abundance daily.*

- *I am financially free! Abundance and prosperity come to me in many ways.*

- *I always have more than enough to share of my riches and of myself. I do believe I am rich$$$ And this is all so!*

- *I rejoice and give thanks for the happiness and riches we all share.*

- *Today I thank God for all the wealth which flows to me, fulfilling all my dreams.*

- *Money and riches come to me in many ways.*

- *Resources flow to me whenever I need them.*

- *I am well supported by the universe. - Wellbeing abounds.*

- *Money is attracted to me easily and effortlessly.*

- *I release all resistance to attracting money.*

- *I am worthy of a positive cash flow!*

- *I celebrate my financial stability. Money flows to me in expected and unexpected ways.*

- *I release any fear of financial success.*

- *I am now open to receiving the abundance this universe has to offer me.*

- *I am grateful for being looked after by the Divine Source.*

- *I am happy and grateful that I have transformed my monthly income into my weekly income.*

- *My higher self and I are both in agreement and are one with <u>tremendous amounts of money</u>.*

- *I am able to accomplish anything I desire.*

- *I am too valuable and worthy to think negative thoughts.*

- *I deserve health, happiness, and success.*

- *I deserve the very best life has to offer me.*

- *I <u>Ask, Believe and Receive</u>.*

- *I am worthy of love and practice self love.*

- *I have faith in myself by having faith in the universe.*

- *I am guided by my desire to serve others.*

- *All financial needs and desires are not only on their way, but will arrive on time and always for my highest good.*

- *I'm as strong as I need to be and can accomplish anything I place by attention upon.*

- *I have within myself all the necessary brainpower needed to fulfill any desires of my choosing.*

- *Money, Wealth, Love and Opportunity surround me at all times.*

- *I welcome and am open to any positive opportunity that comes my way today.*

- *I have all that I will ever want or need right here right now.*

- *I acknowledge my blessings from the Divine.*

- *I feel life flowing though me, experiencing its lavish expression.*

- *I open my mind to receive my good knowing nothing is too good to be true or have happen.*

- *As I give fearlessly into life, life gives back to me with magnificent increase.*

- *I let go of past outdated beliefs.*

- *I know that the Divine will always provide.*

- *Whatever assistance I need to guide me is available right now for the asking and is on its way.*

HOW TO USE SIDDIS

Siddis are similar to affirmations. However they are experienced as a form of frequency To use a Siddi, repeat it and allow it to resonate in your mind, and as it does so, experience the meaning of the words as a type of frequency or mental tone.

THE KANAKDHARA SIDDHI

The KANAKDHARA siddhi is said to be a yantra (which is a

series of 36 squares with the mantra written in the squares) and is said to allow one to acquire immense and unlimited wealth.

CHAPTER 31
CHOOSING MENTORS

A mentor should be a person that has already accomplished what you want to accomplish or is on their way to accomplishing something greater. When you establish a good relationship with a mentor, they can be an invaluable source of inspiration and experience e. Mentors avoid one from becoming too comfortable and staying with the familiar by taming our ego. Find a mentor that you feel will make you grow.

A good mentor will shorten the learning curve of success for any facet in life. You will know you have found the right mentor because they will strike a chord or resonate with you. The way a person spends their money is a strong indicator of their values. Money is an amplifier of character. Some people invest to improve their lives and the lives around them. Others spend for selfish reasons. Hence, this quickly determines if a mentor is right for you. *Motivational Mentors throughout the modern age -*

Abraham Hicks	John Grey
Bob Proctor	Kevin Nations
Brian Tracy	Les Brown
Carole Doré	Louise Lynn Hay
Charles D' Angelo	Michael Bernoff
Christopher Howard	Michael Heppell
Dale Carnegie	Napoleon

Deepak Chopra	Oprah Winfrey
Earl Nightingale	Robert Kiyosaki
Frank Hern	Robin Sharma
Garrett J. White	Sam Warrington
Jack Canfield	Scott Rauvers
James Allen	Tony Robbins
Jim Rohn	Wallace D. Wattles
John Assaraf	Dr. Wayne Dywer
	Zig Ziglar

THE BEST ONLINE MENTORS

These people share their knowledge and information and talk about how they made it to the top financially. Some popular Online Mentors include -

Tai Lopez, Gary Vaynerchuk, Tim Sykes, Dave Ramsey, Grant Cardone, Pat Flynn, Tony Robbins, and Tim Ferriss. There is also a video titled **Prosperity Consciousness**, which is very inspiring to watch that can be found online.

TED TALKS - Ted Talks are a series of lectures in front of a live public audience that involves a person who has undergone a challenge and succeeded. They are tremendously inspiring to watch.

ONLINE MASTER CLASSES – These are classes of all types from acting to singing held by seasoned professionals, many of whom have been practicing their profession for decades.

CHAPTER 32
WHY SURRENDERING TO A HIGHER POWER HELPS RESTORE FLOW

SURRENDERING

Praying is an act of surrender, because one prays to get out of circumstances which are out of one's control or one may pray to see a desire realized. Many people who have suffered from drug or alcohol addiction have surrendered to a higher power by turning their problems over to the higher power while passionately believing they can be cured. It takes courage to admit defeat, yet the reward is that one realizes change is possible. Learning to let go can affirm to the universe that you are not big enough to do it all alone and that a higher, more powerful force can create positive lasting change.

SURRENDERING AFFIRMATIONS

- I am open to surrendering to the all-creating force that is responsible for giving life to form, and allow myself to be lived by it, rather than my living it.

- This is not up to me and I don't have any power to force change.

- I surrender to this. I have the power to know the truth about who I truly am and what **IS** possible.

- The Universe always delivers when I allow myself to let

go, abandon struggle and trust in it.

THE MOST EFFECTIVE TIPS FOR EFFECTIVE PRAYER

Our senses cannot experience the Divine, but we can communicate with it. Prayer is one example.

Praying is an act of RECOGNIZING what's important.

As a side note, Decreeing has more power than prayer because a decree is faith and authority attached to the words spoken. All decrees should be made in the first person..

Prayer can be a great form of self-therapy because it acts as a release mechanism for emotions.

Prayers are answered in direct proportion to the amount of sincerity one places in their words. The God within each and every one of us resides in our heart. Pray to your heart to amplify your prayer. Use these prayer tips to magnify your prayer requests -

* Ask yourself " *What is most important to me at this time?*' and pray based on that.

* While praying, allow prayer to **REACH DEEP** down into Spirit.

* Say the words with **meaning**.

* Ask yourself - " *What do I care about the most at this very moment?*". Than pray based on what you care about the most.

* Pray with conviction.

* Pray as if you were the source from which you came.

* Praying in Thankfulness. For Example - " *Thank you universe for now blessing me with unexpected financial abundance.*" or " *Thank you universe for blessing me with immediate, infinite*

financial gain"

CREATING A PRAYER JOURNAL

Some people may find prayer difficult because their mind is *"too busy"*. The antidote to this is to create a prayer journal. Get creative!. Instead of just buying a journal, visit your local crafts store and install dividers, separating each sub-heading you want to pray about. Cut out pictures from magazines that represent your prayers. You can also use yellow post it sticky notes that represent your prayers in your prayer journal.

WORSHIP MUSIC

Listening to music related to your faith before praying can help one pray more effectively. Christians for example like to listen to gospel music before prayer.

A TECHNIQUE TO QUIET THE MIND

To calm a busy mind or slow down racing thoughts, visualize the heat control knob on a stove, or the temperature dial on a thermostat. Next imagine your hand slowly turning down the dial and as you do so, imagine your mental noise becoming reduced as you turn the dial down to a manageable level.

> ➤ **Affirmation** - *When I change the way I see things, the things I see change.*
> ➤ **Affirmation** - *Everyday I demand more from myself than anybody else could humanly expect*

THE 30 DAY VISION BOARD CHALLENGE

The Laws of Abundance are directly tied to the Laws of the Universe. This is because every action creates an equal and opposite reaction. Hence, when one applies those laws one cannot experience anything but abundance and prosperity. A vision board aligns one with their desire and can be a great way to help keep focused on your goal. A vision board helps one become vigilant to their subconscious programming, creating a new habitual lifestyle.

HOW TO INCREASE YOUR FOCUS AND CONCENTRATION

The secret of the power of concentration lies in simply performing tasks for its own sake.

This next technique is used by professional baseball players to create laser sharp focus. On a blank sheet of paper draw a grid of squares totaling 100 squares. Next fill in the squares the numbers 0 to 99 at random intervals in the squares. Next cross out each number in consecutive order starting at number 1 and ending at 99. What will happen is your mind will start to become "stuck" as you do the exercise. The key is to not get frustrated. Instead persist until you reach 99. Do this again with another sheet of paper with grid numbers on it. After you have got good at this exercise, do the exercise again but use a countdown timer and try to do the task faster each time. Next challenge yourself to do the task in a noisy environment such as having a talk radio show on in the background or outdoors. This will help strengthen your mind when distractions are present and create laser focus and sustained concentration.

DEFINE YOUR EXPECTATION OF WEALTH

Key Points -

1 - Define what abundance **MEANS** to you.

2 - Write out all the SPECIFICS of your ideal lifestyle.

3 - Initiate a bold plan of action to take you there.

Because the subconscious mind loves details, first define the true meaning of wealth, what it means to you. Write it out on paper. Create your ideal lifestyle, involving all the costs necessary to maintain it. Be specific, writing down the exact amount to the dollar. This includes necessary expenses you'll pay once you reach your goal. For example, if you want to purchase a yacht, know the slippage fees and the upkeep necessary to keep a yacht. Be as specific as possible and figure out exactly how much you want to manifest. Create a compelling reason for your goal remembering that clarity is key. *For Example* –

1 - I want to have enough money working for me by age _____ in order to provide me the income I will require to live the good life.

2 - Next cut out pictures from magazines that relate to your goal and glue them onto a piece of cardboard. Put your vision board where you will see it every day such as on the refrigerator or on an office note board.

3 - For the next 30 days as you glance at your vision board each day, ask yourself the following question "***What can I do today to make this vision a reality?***". Think of small steps / action that you can implement to follow through on the answer. Know that as you look at the board, know that you must become what you think about because it is the Law of the Universe that you become what you believe.

As you look at your vision board, know you must want to become part of the 5% of people who are financially independent by age 65. Add sincerity and faith to your actions; knowing that persistence supports faith. Avoid becoming obsessed how your vision will manifest; leave the little details to the universe.

ACT!!! & THINK AS THOUGH IT WERE IMPOSSIBLE TO FAIL

If anytime during the next 30 days you become overwhelmed by negative thinking, start a new vision board from scratch. This is the only way to stop negative thoughts destroying your vision. Remember if you need to destroy your vision board, KNOW that you are not destroying your dream, but removing negative thoughts that will infect its chances of success. The new energy you put into creating a new vision board is positive energy, making your new vision board less susceptible to negative thought patterns.

Do things that keep you inspired during the next 30 days. To eliminate worry and fear - Hold your goal clearly in your mind and have faith in yourself by having faith in the universe.

**Unexpected circumstances that are beyond our control abolish
fear and hesitation because we are forced to
adapt and develop solutions.**

CHAPTER 33
TECHINQUES THAT STRENGTHEN ONE'S CONNECTION TO THE CREATIVE MIND

THE ORIGINATING AND PARENT MINDS

Our whole universe was conceived purely though mental power or thought and our mental power is in kind with that of the Parent Mind. We have within us creative power because our mind exists as a mere thought of the Parent Mind. Hence, making the conscious choice to experience aliveness and creative power manifests our desires. As long as one remembers that thought is in direct proportion to how we perceive our relationship to the Parent Mind, one will always understand how the powers of manifestation operate.

THE PARENT MIND

The Parent Mind is also known as **THE CREATOR**, the **ONE** or the **ULTIMATE DIVINE MIND**. Our conscious mind exists as a mere thought of the Great Parent Mind and as long as this **KNOWING** exists in one's consciousness, you will exist, for you are it. Because we exist as a part of the Divine, it is impossible to be separated from the one true Parent Mind which is always seeking continuous expression through us. Any separation is due to our own ignorance.

If the substance of our thoughts contain such creative power, why than are we hampered by such adverse conditions or feel powerless at times? This is because we use our power inadvertently because at the very starting point of thought, we allow it to be influenced by external conditions. This in turn causes a self-repeating cycle of events to take place, which occur due to an erroneous belief system. This in turn causes one to live their lives based upon outdated beliefs. The antidote to this is to get to the core beliefs about money, relationships or whatever is causing the hardship, struggle or regret. Re-programmed beliefs now allow one to begin the use of their mental power at a newly revised starting point because the thoughts are coming from a revised core of belief. This is why it is key to re-evaluate one's belief system when moving up the ladder of success.

This force is constantly flowing and working through our minds; thinking through our mind. To experience this for yourself, begin by allowing your mind to act as a clear channel for this mode of operation, allowing it to conform to the generic lines of Spirit. Some may fear doing this because they may feel a loss of their sense of individuality. However, if one only tries they soon discover that they end up strengthening their powers of manifestation by KNOWING that they are sharing and PARTICIPATING in the great work of **CREATION** itself.

CHAPTER 34
GUIDED MEDITATIONS FOR MANIFESTING WEALTH AND ABUNDANCE

You can record the mental visualization exercises shown in this chapter to your MP3 player using your computer or on to a CD and create guided visualizations to playback and listen to or you can just read over them and perform the steps as shown in the following pages.

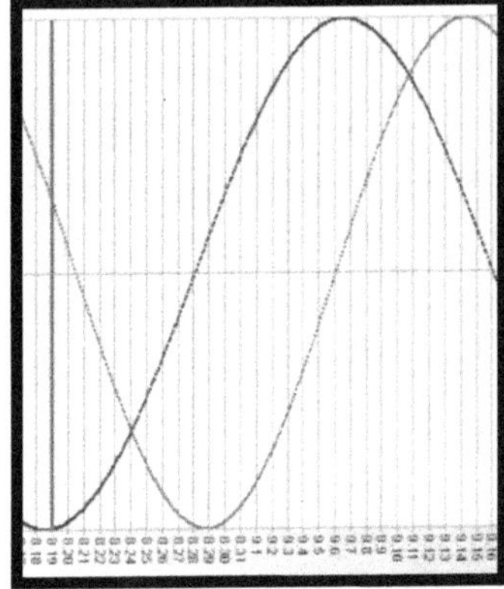

For an added boost, try performing the Guided Imagery Exercises / Energetic Clearing during your peak Intuitive and / or Intellectual Biorhythm cycles are peaking. Repetition forms belief. Repetition forms crests and waves of energy, which form a habit. The energy from habits and beliefs fills what I term "cups" in a part of our brain. When the energy in this cup begins to peak and crest, it manifests experiences and draws to us circumstances. It may be that at the peak of a Biorhythm cycle, that when the right state of mind is present, that it manifests our goals and desires more rapidly than usual. You can find numerous Biorhythm charts for free online. Just be sure to find one that has the Intuitive / Intellectual Biorhythm listing.

The first guided imagery exercise shown below consists of visualizing 2 separate TV screens which are suspended upon a series of strings, like a puppet. These TV screens are a representation of your ideal lifestyle. It is much easier for the mind to observe activity taking place on a television screen rather than trying to feel the activity.

1 - Relax your mind and body.

2 - Next imagine your body being drawn, moved back in time if you will to the time you were young, smaller, lighter and

shorter.

3 - **Picture Television Screen #1** - On this television screen suspended above concrete with strings, see on the screen a time in your youth when you were between 2 and 7 years of age, and identify periods during that time that you identified as important; turning points if you will. These are times that have to do with how, why when and where you picked up beliefs about money.

4 - Become aware of the words your ears heard and the thoughts that formed in your mind when it came to interpreting your definition about money. Hear, feel and see exactly what you experienced back at that time. What are you hearing, seeing and feeling? What are you experiencing? Experience it like it was yesterday. See hear and experience with the intellect of a child, trying to make sense of those words and feelings.

5 - **Television Screen #2** - Next to television screen #1, see a second television screen also suspended by strings. On this screen you see yourself at another crucial juncture point in your early years listening to words about money. What are you hearing? What are people showing to you, presenting to you about money that has shaped your current existing beliefs about money. Is it daytime, nighttime, or are you inside or outside?

Be as specific to the details as possible. Fearlessly and effortlessly look at all the details and parts. Examples include: I had to wear second-hand clothes. I drove an old beat up car. I was never able to properly invest. I could never pay my rent etc. Or the belief that you do not deserve money or that you are not worthy of receiving an abundance of money or that you don't know how to earn money. Maybe you are embarrassed that you don't have enough. Or embarrassed of having too much.

Most important of all, what are you doing, seeing, hearing, feeling and experiencing exactly at that crucial turning point in your life that caused your current scarcity mindset. Experience those feelings of being scared to spend money / wisely invest. One must learn to experience their feelings as truthfully as possible in order to dissolve abundance blocks. Stay, see, hear and feel these scenes as vividly as possible.

6 - Identify the most significant scenes of all that has impacted, impacted and shaped and formed your relationship about money.

7 - Next ask yourself - "*How did these scenes affect and influence me? What did those scenes cost me? or do to me?" What was the impression they left me with?* "

8 - Next imagine yourself moving around, looking over and around and right through both scenes of the TV screen. Allow yourself to understand these scenes, knowing that **UNDERSTANDING** how those scenes affected you actually created its own form of power over you.

9 - Next clearly KNOW that you formed your current existing beliefs about money which shaped and influenced your relationship with money while you were only just a few years of age. As a matter of fact you formed these relationships about money over the course of a long period of time. UNDERSTAND that you were too young to know then what you know now and that beliefs change over time.

10 - Return to Screen #1 - Next STATE YOUR INTENTION to break out of these false and outdated belief systems. Repeat out loud so the words affect your subconscious - "*That is not me because* _________________________."

11 - Next imagine yourself holding up a pair of large pliers. See the pliers cutting the strings holding Television screen #1. As the television begins falling, feel, see and hear the glass shattering into thousands of tiny fragments as it encounters the cold hard concrete. See all scenes, past experiences and erroneous beliefs about money erasing themselves while it does so.

12 - Return to Screen #2 - Next repeat out loud so the words affect your subconscious - "*That will never, ever be me ever again because* _________________________."

13 - Next see yourself cutting the strings holding Television screen #2. As it plummets towards the ground, feel, see and hear the glass shattering. See the scenes becoming erased as the glass shatters into a thousand tiny pieces.

14 - Repeat out loud - "*That's not me because I am no longer 5 years old. I am no longer in that scene. I no longer live that life. I choose to no longer tolerate its power over me. I can make as much money as I choose to. I don't live that life. I am no longer in these scenes.*"

YOUR FUTURE RE-DEFINED

15 - Next picture yourself in the future with immense wealth. See all the good your wealth is doing for the world. Who you benefit. What kind of role model are you? Who are you helping? Who are you assisting and serving?

16 - Experience your new relationship with money and see it as a never ending cycle, flowing in and out of your life; from the value you give, treating it with respect.

SUMMARY

UNDERSTANDING brings to the REALIZATION that experiencing a past belief gives one the power to transform it. This is how EFT (*Emotional Freedom Technique*) works. One simply experiences a past trauma, while at the same time experiences deep acceptance for themselves which causes the trauma to no longer hold its power over the person.

Faith based upon understanding gives one confidence to push beyond fear and out of one's comfort zone. This exercise allows you to understand that as you experience yourself at a younger age, you were forced to pick up other people's beliefs about money. Since that time, you have learned to recognize your talents, experience and perfect your gifts and come to know and understand WHO YOU **TRULY ARE**. You now no longer tolerate the beliefs you formed early on. You now

RECOGNIZE that you have the freedom to make whatever choices you want regarding your beliefs; <u>allowing your new beliefs to make you</u>. You deserve respect, love and happiness and to enjoy a life filled with satisfaction, fulfillment and prosperity and most of all to enjoy every moment of it!!!

WHO YOU TRULY ARE

You are abundant - you are wealthy - you are rich - you live an abundant life - **you MATTER.**

GUIDED IMAGERY ROADMAP TO WEALTH EXERCISE #2

These next 2 guided visualization exercises are used by the top money block removal practitioners which has helped thousands of people. It restores order by reprogramming old belief patterns that have become disordered and help one connect with the millionaire blueprint their higher self.

When you allow your feelings to change through visualization or guided imagery, you begin to feel different on the inside. This is because you are creating a new oscillating frequency which changes what you will experience / invites new experiences into your waking reality.

THE MILLION DOLLAR FEEING TECHINQUE -

Our feelings cultivate how we experience the receiving of money. There is no difference between receiving $100 and $1 million dollars. If you ask any millionaire how they felt when they made their first $1 million dollars, they will tell you that they felt ordinary and not overly excited; that it was just a number for them. This next guided imagery exercise involves connecting with your higher self in order to align yourself with the future millionaire version of yourself.

1 - Close your eyes and ask yourself " *What would it feel like to me if I actually manifested $1 million dollars right now?*' or "*How do I feel when aligning myself with the million dollar version of me?*"

2 - Next set an alarm to ring each hour each day and when the

alarm sounds, visualize in your mind for just 1 or 2 minutes what it would FEEL like having $1 million.

The success to this technique is lots of small visualizations spread out throughout the day for 2 to 5 minutes each day generates feelings of monetary success, which attracts to you your goal. The next time you see an expensive car, luxury yacht or home, imagine yourself stepping into the millionaire version of yourself and you will feel your wealth vibration rise and you will feel empowered. Now let's explore a more in-depth method of experiencing the million dollar version of yourself which utilizes the power of your higher self.

WHAT IS THE HIGHER SELF?

Because our higher self is connected to our future higher self, it already knows what's best for us. Your higher self speaks to you through subtle impulses and the sooner you follow through on these impulses without hesitation or doubt, the better off you'll be.

The best way to explain how your higher self is connected to your future subconscious mind is to imagine 2 telephones. Instead of being connected to one another by physical distance, think of them being connected with one another through time, in this case going from the present to the future. This is why our higher self guides us on our life path and purpose because it has learned to transit information between these 2 points in time (the present and the future). This is just one of the many attributes of the higher self and the full explanation of the higher self's purpose is outside the scope of this book.

When you thank your higher self for being in the right place at the right time or for experiencing acts of spontaneous synchronicity, you will receive more of the same.

Now let's take a look at this next exercise -
THE MILLION DOLLAR FEEING TECHINQUE #2

1 - Relax your body and perform a grounding exercise to ground into your space.

2 - On a mental level, call in and activate the millionaire dollar / abundant version of yourself, allowing you to live in complete abundance in every single area of your life. This can be done by imagining yourself coming across something you desire such as a brand new Ferrari and asking yourself - *"How would the millionaire version of me look after and drive this car?"*

3 - Imagine now in your mind a giant TV screen in front of you. As you look at the screen, you see a movie playing on it. The movie is you living the million dollar version of yourself.

4 - As you watch the movie, become fully aware of what is happening in the movie. What are you doing? See all the details as clear as possible.

5 - Next *"jump!"* into the movie screen and allow yourself to witness the movie through your own eyes. Be aware of feelings, thoughts, sensations and sounds.

6 - At this time you will start to **notice different sensations in your body**. You begin feeling different (*good*). As you feel this, you feel a shift in your thoughts as you no longer choose to tolerate old thought patterns that were holding you back.

7 - Feel these new changes occurring right down to the cellular level.

8 - Next imagine clearing out past distorted energy from family generational lines that have caused old outdated beliefs. Imagine these being cleared 7 generations back, and 7 generations into the future, restoring Divine Order.

9 - Re-relax your body.

10 - Remind yourself that lack, worry, fear and doubt are not part of your future nor are they a part of your true essence of WHO YOU TRULY ARE.

11 - Now return to the movie screen as you live the movie through your eyes and imagine a ball of golden light right above you. As this ball of light approaches you, you see it is your HIGHER SELF returning from the future.

12 - Next ALLOW your **FUTURE HIGHER** SELF to simply drop down through your head, into your body, going down vertically into your heart and merging with your higher self that exists in the present. See these both merge into one form, allowing the new form to be molded and coded with the energy of this new movie into each and every cell of your body.

13 - Next *jump out!!!* of the movie screen and witness the movie from the outside. As you watch the movie, make any final adjustments or additions you need to make to the movie to make this movie perfect, divine and as it is meant to be for you right now.

14 - Next return to the movie screen and witness it surrounded with golden light and see it transform itself into a ball of golden light. Let the ball of golden light approach the top of your head and drop down vertically into your heart just as it did before.

15 - Next see the ball of golden light implode in your heart. As the energy floods every single cell of your being, allow every single cell of your body to become re-coded with the **TRUTH** of **THE FUTURE** that you are choosing to step into.

16 - Allow your new vibration to expand and grow allowing the vibrations to be felt by divine beings.

17 - Next meditate upon gratitude, appreciation and thankfulness.

18 – Now return to the present; opening your eyes.

LEARNING TO LIVE INTO THE MILLIONIARE VERSION OF YOURSELF

This is a great exercise to do after the previous exercise because it enhances the ability for you to step into the millionaire version of yourself.. Ask yourself - "*What would the new version of me do?*" or "*Now that I am the millionaire version of me, how can I step up and participate?*" Affirm this from a place of aligned action.

ARCHITECTURAL **ENERGETIC** ARCHITECTURE EXERCISE #3

1 - Close your eyes, relax and imagine the light of your consciousness rising out of your body until it is 300 feet above you. Feel, sense and sense this light.

2 - Allow this light to stream down, flowing in through the top of your head. See this light as pure **TRUTH** and **ABUNDANCE**; the truth of who **YOU REALLY ARE - KNOWING** that abundance is your natural birthright.

3 - Allow this light to flood all 5 senses; seeing, hearing, touching, feeling and tasting.

4 - Allow this light to enter your throat than down into your heart.

5 - Next see it enter your solar plexus, washing out all fear, anxiety, doubt and shame.

6 - Next allow it to enter your stomach region, washing out anywhere you feel disempowered.

7 - Next see the energy enter your root area, which is near the bottom part of your body, and allow yourself to stand in your birthright of abundance.

8 - Allow this energy to flow down through your legs, knees, feet and eventually to the center of the planet. Allow yourself to feel safe, secure, supported and loved as you connect to the center of the earth, becoming one with it.

9 - Next bring this energy back up through your body, settling in

your heart region and allow the energy to expand outwards from your heart. Imagine it radiating out, EXPANDING 360 degrees in all directions. Allow the energy to expand in layers; first 10ft, 20ft and up to a maximum of 40ft.

10 - Now think to yourself at what age you first thought you did not have enough money. Allow the first answer that pops into your mind to be the right one, because it usually is. When was the very first time at an early age that you felt a vibration or pattern that you did not have enough money? Did this energy come from authority figures such as parents, authority figures of your religion, teachers or others? FEEL this energy as it begins to appear around your body.

11 - Now tune into the vibration of lack (*or area that feels dark*) and point to the exact part (*or regions*) on your body that feel heavy and sluggish.

12 - Now ask yourself - "***What is the main emotion I am feeling right now that is tied to this vibration?***"

13 - Now replace that vibrational space with as much light as you feel comfortable with. ALLOW this white light to fill in and transmute unwanted vibrations. As this light fills in these **"holes"**, see it transmuting the low vibrations across all dimensions, time, space and alternate realities. ALLOW the light to vaporize / transmute any remaining negative "*dark energy*".

14 - Return now to when you were younger, experiencing any feelings / thoughts of where you did not have enough money or felt that you were not supported by the universe or no one was there when you needed him / her the most / feelings of abandonment etc.

15 - Ask yourself "*What was my mom's main story about money?" Did she see the plenty that already exists? What was her main emotion about money?*"

16 - Ask yourself - "*At what age did I begin playing out /*

duplicating these patterns about money? and what is now my main perception about money?"

17 - As you ask yourself these questions, **ALLOW** yourself to become aware of any heaviness, tightness or feelings of contraction that may become relevant. As you do so, tune into each region one at a time, filling it with pure **WHITE LIGHT**.

18 - Accept the fact that money blocks occur because you are duplicating this energy which you carried on over from your mom because you saw her as the authority at the time. Any other emotions you have tied to this, send in the light and feel it clearing and transmuting the low, heavy blockages and vibrations.

19 - Now do the same with your father's beliefs about money.

20 - KNOW anywhere and everywhere that you are living life that duplicated and carried on over to your consciousness beliefs about money when you were younger. KNOW this is contradictory to **WHO YOU REALLY ARE**. KNOWING now that abundance is your natural birthright.

21 - Any other patterns you FEEL are holding you back, allow them to be transmuted by the energy of the white light.

22 - If you feel any other spaces that need filling, fill them with the light of TRUTH.

23 - Ask yourself the question - "*What would it take for me to have it all? To be fully self-sufficient, supported, to have enough and to have MORE THAN ENOUGH?"*

Notes –
You may hear, see or feel the "dark" areas which need to be filled in by the light.

Another powerful technique is instead of using just white light, ask yourself "*What is the appropriate color for this region of the body?"* The first color that pops into your mind is the correct one. Next send that color to the area that needs it and repeat with the next area.

You may also want to use this color question for healing by

asking yourself. *"What color does this part of my body need right now in order to heal Itself?"* If healing another person, you can intuitively feel what color they need for healing, or if possible ask them what color they feel drawn to.

SUMMARY

You don't have to perform every single step of every exercise. You can modify the exercises to your liking. If you don't get satisfactory results, than revise the exercise until you feel you are achieving the results you want. You can do this with any of the techniques outlined in this book. What works for one person, may not work for another. These exercises only serve to show you the **BASIC FUNDAMENTALS** that have been proven to work over the years as used by experts who have removed money blocks from thousands of people.

CHAPTER 35
LEARNING TO CONNECT WITH SOURCE TO EXPERIENCE IMPROVED HEALTH AND VITALITY

The ego could learn a lot from the body, but rarely does. Instead it is your higher self that knows how to look after your body. It is only when we lose our connection to it, that we stray down the path that causes us to experience lack, illness or misfortune.

The ego has only 2 things to offer - feeling good or feeling bad

WHY A PHYSICAL LACK OF ENERGY IS AN ILLUSION

A lack of energy comes from a lack of motivation, unless of course you have a medical condition. Did you know that we use just 10% of our brain, not to mention the bulk amount of energy in our body that goes unused.

Scientists calculated that if the electrical power of hydrogen atoms contained in the human body could be harnessed, that they would be able to power the electrical needs of the United States for almost an entire week. And some people complain that they don't have any energy!!!

A strong and clear Spiritual Connection to something you believe in the most also helps keep one motivated. Detoxification of heavy metals from the body is also key to maintaining good physical energy levels. If you unexpectedly feel fatigued, it may be from the toxic metals that occur in the food you eat. Mercury in fish is one example. If you are vegetarian and you lack energy, you need more plant proteins (beans, Chia Seeds or French lentils) and iron (blackstrap molasses or spinach).

Definition of Optimization - The highest and best use of results that come from the efforts put forth regarding your time.

Did you know? Every square inch on the surface of the human body experiences 15 pounds pushing upon it from air in the atmosphere.

The cellular processes in your body turn over millions of cells each and every second; absorbing the nutrients from the food you eat while at the same time discarding waste they have received from their environment such as food, air and water. Hence, if your thought patterns are one of disease or lack, and thoughts permeate the environment, as your cells continue to turn over, eventually over time, your negative thoughts will merge with this process, contributing to dis-ease because your thoughts are not in equilibrium with the vibration of feeling alive   and   whole.

Health is about listening to the subtle messages your body is telling you. Your body knows how to look after itself; you need only listen. These impulses that guide our health can become distorted if our ego causes us to live from a mindset of ignorance and neglect. The messages your body may be telling you include - to avoid certain situations, create a change in lifestyle, or to avoid or eat certain kinds of foods.

THE EGO (Everybody's Got One)

Definition of the Ego - An exaggerated sense of self importance.

What wealth self-improvement book would be without a section on the Ego? Today, as our civilization moves towards a more educated and modern environment, the ego is still sensitive to any perceived threats. It is a fact that 99% of all things we perceive as threats turn out to be non-threatening. Think of the Ego as an outdated security system. It only wants to protect and make us feel good by staying with the familiar. The Ego cannot catch up to the moment, which is why learning to experience the moment allows one to rise above their ego. Those with inflated egos make favorite targets by critics.

Your ego constantly wants more, more and more. Hence

you subconsciously end up creating more of what you define as "*success*" in order to satisfy the ego's thirst for more.

4 ANTIDOTES TO RELINQUISHING CONTROL OF THE EGO

KINDNESS AND COMPASSION
The last 4 letters of Compassion spell **PASSION**.

Definition of Compassion - Wanting more for others, than you want for yourself.

When one can embrace another beyond concern for themselves, wishing more for others then what they wish for themselves, they are practicing true compassion. As you practice this often enough, you will soon discover that you will experience an abundance of friendly, helpful people who want to assist you in your pursuits.

The success of a community is determined by the amount of compassion expressed by its inhabitants

KINDNESS
Kindness allows one to detach from ego orientated desires; affording one a clear connection with the rhythm of the universe. When one can exert compassion when life gives you challenges, the less you are to blame other people for your own shortcomings.

AWARENESS
Awareness elevates you to you experiencing your authentic true self. You no longer have to explain your missed opportunities or shortcomings.

A TECHNIQUE FOR GETTING MORE ENERGY OUT OF FOOD

One way to test this for yourself is before you take a power nutrition bar, or health supplement or anti-aging supplement; before you eat it, hold it in your hands and mentally say - "*I allow myself to experience vibrancy, vitality, energy and health*". Now eat the food. You will find that when you eat the food after performing this technique, that you will feel much more energized compared to eating the food without the technique. This technique works extremely well with water, because water is easily affected by intention, as shown in numerous experiments by **Dr. Emoto** and **Dr. Tiller** of Stanford University.

References

Double-blind test of the effects of distant intention on water crystal formation. Radin D et al. Sept 2006.

Can an aspect of consciousness be imprinted into an electronic device? Tiller WA et al. Apr 2000.

As our planet rotates throughout space, it becomes bathed in a universal energy that permeates all. This energy has its own innate natural ability to restore order and balance to all the cells of our body. One way to feel and connect with this energy is to simply relax, calm the mind and let go and *allow*. As you let go of all worry and doubt your mind will naturally enter this flow.

Emotions such as humor and truth return one's state of mind to order and harmony and can speed the rate at which healing occurs. Learn to laugh at your mistakes and failures, have a healthy sense of humor about your defects, accept your limitations and allow yourself to be who you truly are. Allow your body's cells to experience child-like feelings of happiness and radiant joy. Celebrate their wondrous divine workings and natural vitality. Just ACKNOWLEDGING these few simple facts works wonders for health and well-being.

As I write this, I am reminded of comedian Steve Martin, in one of his very first movies called **The Jerk**. You can see in the movie he is obviously new at acting. However this has given him the advantage in that he had so much fun while making the movie. The movie earned $100 million worldwide, and cost just $4 million to make.

SUMMARY

Taking common sense precautions, listening to your intuition and your body's subtle messages are all that is necessary to keep you safe and healthy and prevent dis-ease.

Wise Words of Wisdom - Civilization is the intelligent management of human emotion

Affirmation - "*I am so happy and grateful now that every molecule and fiber of my being is vibrating in perfect harmony with God's Laws. My whole body is getting healthier and stronger and more vibrant every minute of every day*!!"

FORGIVENESS

It has been said that **resentment acts as the catalyst for cancer**. The antidote for resentment is forgiveness. Forgiveness releases stagnant emotions such as judgment and other low, dark emotions leaving one with an inner sense of peace and calm. This allows one to begin living in the moment which generates feelings of Wholeness; which is where all healing comes from.

WHY FEELINGS OF PROSPERITY CAN ENHANCE FEELINGS OF WELL-BEING

In many cases, people have found that when they released their blockages that were stopping them from experiencing prosperity and abundance, that they experienced improved health. This is because abundance consciousness creates feelings of well-being, ease and allowing, all of which are some of the strongest emotions in the universe.

It has been my experience that unexpected knee pain comes from unresolved internal emotional issues or conflicts such as guilt, repressed anger or an inability to forgive. After releasing these emotions, the pain ceases to exist or a spontaneous healing may occur. Now that we have scientific confirmation that our thoughts influence our biology (*as shown in Chapter* 1) we may soon learn that repressed feelings or emotions are also affecting our financial health.

Small minds discuss people, mediocre minds discuss events and great minds discuss ideas.

CHAPTER 36
PRE-EMPTIVE LESSONS

MUST BE LEARNED / EXERCISED. WHY PRE-EMPTIVE LESSONS ARE EASIER THAN LIFE LESSONS

We are all on the same Spiritual path. It is much better to recognize the divine laws of the universe at large in advance rather than living in ignorance and having to suffer the consequences.

When we are born, we have lessons in life that teach us to value certain virtues. These lessons depend upon our current state of Spiritual attainment at the time we are born. The most common values are Love, Appreciation, Respect for Life and Gratitude. When you sincerely **PRACTICE** these virtues, you can ***usually*** avoid unnecessary struggle and future hardship. However; even by practicing these values, life wants us to learn more because life flows through us and wants to evolve to higher forms of expression. Below is a partial list of virtues. The list is by no means complete. The list can be a great way to pre-learn learn life's lessons.

- Forgiveness and self-forgiveness. Forgiving yourself is one of the best ways to experience healing and inner peace.

- **KNOWING** that you are **WORTHY** and deserving of infinite blessings and that abundance is your natural birthright.

- To be thankful. Be thankful for even the smallest things,

no matter how insignificant they may seem.

- Avoiding Temptation. Creates Inner strength.

- Trusting in Intuition. Creates trust in the universe.

- Watching out for negative thoughts. Avoids self-sabotage and regret.

- Believing in oneself

- Refusing to play the role of victim

- Keeping Balance in all things

- To master your divine gifts and talents to their fullest

- To remain humble while triumphant because it is the humble that are secure

- To be Compassionate. Because it assists the harmony in the world.

Chapter 37
BUDGETING TECHNIQUES

When you create a budget plan and adhere to it, you keep track of future expenses and will find it much easier to save your money. This gives you confidence that you are in control of your finances. Drafting a budget works best as soon as you receive your paycheck or other lump sum of money. The more confidence you have over the control of your spending, the less likely the ego is tempted into wasting it on unnecessary things.

Keeping track of one's spending habits is the best way to create savings confidence. Make a commitment to draft up a budget every time you receive a lump sum of money. It is inevitable that minor expenses will unexpectedly pop up each month. Even when an unexpected expense shows up, you will discover that you still have control over your spending habits.

KNOW that the minor concession of adhering to a budget plan does not feel as bad as experiencing the pain of regret of not being able to save money. Life teaches us that short term

Nothing in life is free. When one pays for something that is worthwhile and lasting, it generates feelings of appreciation

sacrifices are necessary if we want to enjoy the rewards we seek. Having peace of mind that an emergency cash slush fund exists to cover one's expenses in time of need is one example. Other examples include saving to purchase a new car, boat or home, or that dream vacation are excellent examples where short to medium term sacrifices are necessary.

SAVING

Because everything begins with thought, which comes from Spirit, when you save money, you should think of your savings as an investment in your protection against future adversity and loss. Savings can also be of benefit if you see a good opportunity that you know looks good and want to invest in it. How regretful would you feel if you did not have the funds to invest when you saw an opportunity that was right for you?

LAYOUT FOR A SIMPLE BUDGET

Writing out monthly expenses allows one to see if they are spending more than they are making. This simple budget plan shown below is made for monthly or bi-monthly expenses and income. On a piece of paper draw the following 4 rows and columns and fill in the columns with the associated headings.

Current Income	Projected Extra Income	Expenses	Current Savings

Totals

Current and Projected Income $_____________________

Total Income minus expenses $_______________________

Total Savings for this month $________________________

In summary, simply deduct your monthly (or bi-weekly) expenses from your monthly income to get the amount left over. Next add any left over money to your current savings.

1 – First add both your current and projected / expected income.

2 - Next deduct your expenses from your total income from the month.

3- With what is left remaining, add this to the savings column.

If you don't have any left over, or are in the - negative you need to make some changes or you will constantly be short of money.

EXPENSE SHEET DETAILS -
Begin with a general outline -
Food
Gasoline
Electric

Food
How much do you intend to pay for food this month? Write down the approximate cost of each item and then total these items.

Gas
How far do you intend to drive this month?

Projected Income
This is unexpected income. Examples include IRS Refund Checks, Paycheck Bonuses, Overtime etc.

Do the same for any expense that you intend to encounter during the month.

A budget plan only works if one makes a serious commitment and sticks to it. Most of all allow for flexibility along the way.

Wise Words of
Wisdom –
Belief tames the
ego, creating
scaffolding that
supports ambition

CHAPTER 38
SUGGESTIONS AND ADVICE FOR AN EASIER LIFE

An old folklore method, thought to be infallible in attracting fortune into one's life, involves the **Holly Bush**. The saying goes that on a rainy day one clasps their hands around the stem of the bush and chants *"Holly Tree, Holly Tree, Let Much Wealth Flow to Me"*.

GO ON A VIRTUAL SHOPPING SPREE

Feelings of satisfaction match the vibration you are seeking. For example, if you go on a virtual online shopping spree, which involves clicking on items and putting them into your online shopping cart and not actually buying the items, you will find that it is a great way to get rid of a scarcity mindset and raise your wealth vibration. Visit websites with items that interest you and add the items to your cart. You don't have to checkout and pay for the items. Just go on a make-believe virtual shopping spree and most of all **HAVE FUN!!**.

HOW TO INTERPRET THE WISDOM RECEIVED FROM DREAMS

Our dreams give us information via symbolism, therefore the pictures and images you receive during your dreams need to be properly interpreted in order to make sense of them. Hence asking the right questions will unpeel the wisdom that is contained within the symbology. One can always remember what they dreamed when they immediately write down what they \dreamed upon awakening. However you can also use a technique to interpret the symbolism that talks to you through your dreams, which is usually filled with expert wisdom and guidance.

A SIMPLE DREAM INTERPRETATION TECHINQUE

1 - After you first wake up after a dream, immediately ask yourself any of the following questions -
"What is this dream trying to tell me?" or

"What is this dream saying to me?" or

"What is the true meaning behind the symbology of this dream(s)?"

2 - Next immediately write down the information that intuitively enters your mind.

If you perform the above process long enough and often enough, soon you will find that you no longer have to ask the question(*s*) because your mind has already learned to interpret your dreams.

How to Receive Clear Insight to Any Problem

Leonardo Da Vinci was an accomplished sculpture craftsman and artist. Leonardo Da Vinci's Genius came from him being able to visualize clearly in his mind working inventions and then clearly sketch out the details on paper in great detail. This technique utilizes a method to help create the same type of effect.

1 - See in your mind your problem

2 - Next imagine your problem in the form of a lump of clay.

3 - Next imagine your hands molding that clay into the solution that you are seeking. Imagine the solution presenting itself in the shape of the clay that you are molding.

4 - Next see your clay sculpture being firm and dry.

5 - Next imagine yourself with a paper and pen in your hand and drawing out the details in the clay. See the solution revealing itself as you sketch onto the pad.

6 - Next imagine yourself putting down your sketch pad and

paper and allowing any free flowing thoughts to enter your mind.

7 - Next pick up a pen and paper and write out what comes into your mind. As you do so, you will find that the answers to your problem will be much more clear and of higher contrast, allowing you to extract the necessary information you need to solve your problem.

YOUR PERSONAL QUANTUM SUCCESS CARD

Cut out a blank card and write on 1 side your goal or stated objective. On the other side of the card write -

Wise Words of Wisdom – If you want to know what something is, first define what it isn't

"*I tell you, that to everyone who has, more will be given; but from him who has not, even what he has will be taken away.*" Luke 19:26, RSV.

or

" *You become what you believe.*"

Carry this card in your wallet and look at it whenever you need inspiration.

UNDERSTANDING THE FUNDAMENTALS OF WEALTH

Fundamentals act as a guide to keep us on the path of what works and what doesn't work. When you understand the fundamentals of something, your success is much more certain. You can learn the fundamentals of just about anything by -

* Reading books
* Taking courses
* Taking classes
* Attending events / conventions
* Seeking the advice of coaches
* Learning from mentors

HOW TO STOP LOSING THINGS

A neat trick to stop losing small objects such as keys etc. Is once you have found it, place the article over your heart and say 3 times "*I love you*". This greatly reduces the number of times the small article becomes lost or is hard to find. You will find you will lose that item far less often or not at all.

RETURNING THE ENERGY OF MONEY BACK TO ONE OF NEUTRALITY

An interesting study conducted in China by Qing Yang and colleagues in November 2012 titled: *Diverging Effects of Clean Versus Dirty Money on Attitudes*, found that when people paid for their food with money that was visibly dirty that they were more likely to be short changed. However, when they paid with notes that appeared new, fresh or crisp, they were treated with more fairness, respect and were less likely to be shortchanged.

The spare change you receive from your supermarket after paying for something has exchanged itself with thousands, perhaps millions of hands. This gives the money its own unique vibration. When money first rolls off the printing presses and is distributed to banks, it is in a purely neutral state. As money enters circulation, it takes on its own unique vibration.

Because money is primarily neutral when it rolls off the printing press, you want to return money you receive back to its neutral state so its neutral vibration can be restored. One way to do this is to place the money in a place it won't be disturbed for a length of time. I personally place spare change in the outdoor sunshine for a minimum of 3 weeks on a small table. Next when you collect and clean the money, hold it up to the sun and say *"I release all resistance to attracting money. I am worthy of a positive cash flow."* You have now programmed the neutral money with a new positive vibration. Next take the money to the bank and exchange it for notes. This puts the now neutral money back into circulation, just as it began when it came out of the mint. You will discover that when you carry the notes around with you that you will feel different.

Affirm - *All of the money that I spend, returns to me multiplied in a never ending cycle of increase and enjoyment!!."*

THE MOST POPULAR MOTIVATIONAL MOTION PICTURE SOUNDTRACKS

- Irene Cara - "Flashdance... What A Feeling"
- Nothing's gonna ever keep you down
- R. Kelly - "I Believe I Can Fly"
- Survivor - "Eye Of The Tiger"
- Eminem - "Lose Yourself"
- Bill Conti - "Gonna Fly Now"
- Idina Menzel - "Let It Go"
- Joe Esposito - "You're The Best Around"
- Smash Mouth - "All Star"
- Public Enemy - "Fight The Power"
- Destiny's Child - "Independent Women Pt. 1"
- Kenny Loggins - "Danger Zone"
- Jon Bon Jovi - "Blaze Of Glory"
- Tegan & Sara w/The Lonely Island - "Everything Is Awesome"

CHAPTER 39
WHY THE MONTHS OF MAY AND JUNE ARE ASSOCIATED WITH WEALTH

The   12   Constellations

As earth revolves around the sun, approximately every 4 weeks the east rising sun (*as we see it from our vantage point one earth*) has a new constellation behind it. This depends upon your latitude or location of where you are on earth. For example,

September is the month associated with the astrological sign of Virgo. If you were to use a Sky map Ap, which you can download for free to an android phone or use a free online sky map, you would see that around September 10th of each month (*in North America*), in the morning as the sun rises, the constellation Virgo is behind the sun. The brightest star in the Virgo constellation is Spica. In my location of Hawaii, Spica undergoes its heliacal rising on October 19th, 2020. Due to precession, a year later Spica will rise at a slightly different time. The reason intuition is enhanced may be due to the helical rising of these stars (*the 4 royal Persian stars*) although further research is needed to verify this hypothesis.

The months of May and June are the months traditionally associated with wealth. During May, in North America, the sun rises with the constellation Taurus, which includes the star cluster the Pleiades. In Astrology, the constellation Taurus is associated with prosperity, wealth and abundance.

Hence, the reason intuition is enhanced may be due to the helical rising of these stars. Intuition is partly responsible for the generation of wealth in one's life.

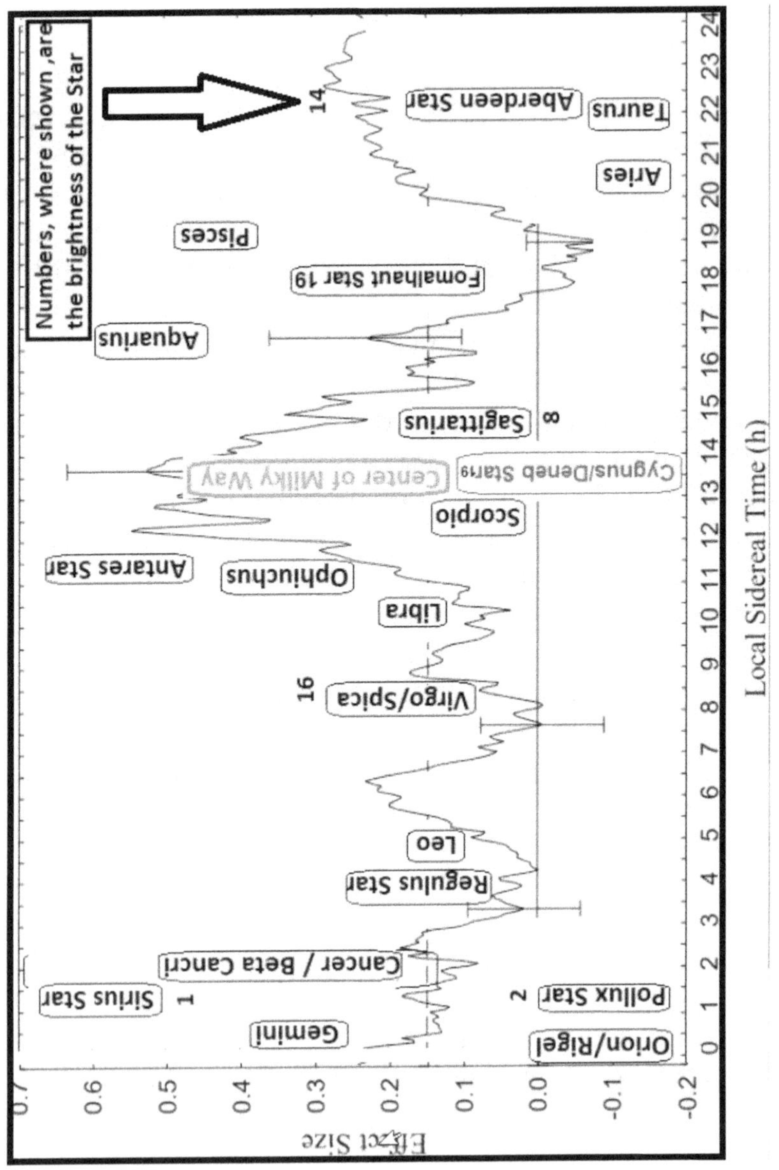
Numbers, where shown, are the brightness of the Star
Sirius Star
Gemini
Cancer / Beta Cancri
Pollux Star
Orion/Rigel
Regulus Star
Leo
Virgo/Spica
Libra
Ophiuchus
Antares Star
Scorpio
Center of Milky Way
Cygnus/Deneb Stars
Sagittarius
Aquarius
Fomalhaut Star 19
Pisces
Aberdeen Star
Taurus
Aries
Effect Size
Local Sidereal Time (h)

Reference

Association Between Effect Size In Free Response Anomalous Cognition Experiments And Local Sidereal Time. *S. James P. Spottiswoode,   Palo   Alto   California.*

What is most interesting is that a study (*shown in the above reference*) showed that precognition/intuition exhibits 4 major peaks each 24 hours (**one peak is shown in the graph above**). These peaks roughly coincide with the 4 Royal Persian Stars. One of these collective intuitive peaks occurs when the star **Aldebaran** (in the Taurus constellation) is rising in the east. What is even more interesting is that the ancient Egyptians would dedicate temples to the helical rising of the star Sirius.

If one looks at the following star chart, one can see that the star Sirius is slightly below Aldebaran, with the Constellation Orion in-between the two.

The so-called **Royal Stars of Persia** are a French invention of the 18th century. They have nothing to do with Persian astrology. The 4 Royal Persian Stars are shown below -

Aldebaran (Taurus Constellation) - (*14th Brightest Star*)

Antares / Deneb (*15th Brightest Star*) / Cygnus (Sagittarius / Galactic Center / Center of the Milky Way Galaxy)

Regulus (Leo Constellation) - (*21st Brightest Star*)

Fomalhaut (Aquarius Constellation)

CHAPTER 40
STRATEGIES FOR BUSINESS SUCCESS

COMPOUND YOUR EFFECTIVENESS
Know what is getting results and allow your success to become compounded. This will greatly enhance the synergy of your success.

USING BUSINESS CARDS TO GROW YOUR BUSINESS

Business cards do work. Their rate of return is between 1% and 3%. In summary, your sales will increase approximately 2.5% for every 2000 cards you pass out. Hence, approximately 88% of business cards handed out will be ignored. You can distribute business cards in person to businesses or place them in the doors of houses, or pay college students to distribute them for you. An average person can distribute up to 200 business cards per day during good weather conditions.

Double sided business cards with the message printed on them *"see other side"* are more cost effective because it does not cost much more to have the second side printed. Also be sure your business card(s) have a compelling reason for people to visit the website, such as offering a free report or a date to act before the coupon or offer expires.

THE DANGERS OF RECEIVING UNEXPECTED FINANCIAL WINDFALLS

People who suddenly receive a large financial windfall have not had time for their vibration to properly adapt to the increase in wealth. They may go out and buy a Ferrari and get in a wreck causing serious injury, or learn to skydive and suffer an accident. The antidote to this is to slowly begin to get used to the large sum(s) of money as it enters your life and be cautious of the risks associated with it.

HOW TO DEAL WITH COPYCATS

There is an old saying that says "*Imitation is the best form of flattery.*"

When someone copies and replicates what you are doing, it is a blessing because it shows that what you are doing is working. One method to outsmarting those who copy you is to create faster, without sacrificing quality, than the other person who is copying

Instead of competing, create

you. Another is to open distributorships and franchises and sign on other people to sell your product or service for you. It is also why patents and copyrights were invented.

TAKING THE TIME TO REVIEW NEW TECHNOLOGIES

Bill Gates has used this technique for years. Every so often he will take time off to review new technology and any new changes. By taking the time to review new ideas, information and technology, it can help one find ways to increase productivity and "catch up" on the latest innovations.

KING SOLOMON'S BUSINESS WISDOM

It is estimated that King Solomon made over a billion dollars a year for more than 40 years and amassed more than a trillion dollars in gold. He was one of the richest men to have ever lived. He has left us with the following wisdom-

1 - Be kind. People don't forget two types of encounters they have with others. 1 - People who are rude. 2 - People who are kind.

2- Choose your friends wisely, they almost always influence the course of your life. A companion of fools suffers harm and misfortune. Surrounding yourself with those who are wise will also make you wise.

3 - Seek out Mentors. A wise group of elders can be of great value because their counsel can help keep you on track and avoid future misfortune. Future plans may not go "*as planned*". By listening to their advice and feedback, projects have a better chance at succeeding because they reduce your learning curve. Also when a bunch of people get together and focus on a single intention, it creates an emergence of ideas.

4- Before you say anything that may not be conductive to the task at hand, ask yourself - "*Do these words improve upon the silence?*"

5 - Be generous. Those who don't give back will end up living a life of want.

6 - What you sow you reap.

7 - Knowledge is more valuable than rubies or pearls. Hence, the saying – "*Give a man a fish and feed him for a day. Teach a man to fish and feed him for the rest of his life*".

8 - Be diligent in all business transactions.

9 - Fortune favors the bold.

10 - Lazy people will always experience poverty.

11 - Be attentive to the needs of your business.

12 - It takes courage to grow, because it shifts you out of your comfort zone. Courage is the featherbed for the soul, helping

one to sleep peacefully at night.

In Folklore, May is the month traditionally associated with wealth.

SPEND TO PROSPER

If you own a business and intuitively feel that certain supplies and equipment are a necessary investment to make your business grow and expand; as you pay for these items, silently affirm in your mind the following -

"I spend to PROSPER without fear, doubt, lack or hesitation."

This is because everything is energy and the energy associated with paying for something **resides in that item**(*s*) for as long as you own it. You want good feelings and vibes in the objects you purchase for your business.

WHY EFFECTIVE
COMMUNICATION IS KEY

The current quality of your business and even your life is determined by how effectively you can communicate with others. This includes how effectively your message comes across in correspondence, videos, conferences and so on.

Effective communication can help create a successful long term relationship. During a job interview, we do our best to communicate our message across to our prospective employer. Having this same effective type of communication with business prospects or when getting our message across in presentations and videos goes a long way to establishing a reputation of quality and how sincere you are. Without effective communication, your clients will soon lose interest in you, no matter how good your product or service may be. Effective communication tools include; e-mail, over the person phone conversations, live teleconferencing, live streaming and more.

THE BASICS OF HEALTHY RELATIONSHIPS

Somebody once wrote - "*Money is like a woman who swore an oath that anybody who did not love her would never have her.*" This means that money commands respect.

Future adversity regarding money can be avoided when one has developed a healthy relationship with money. You can find out if your relationship is strained if you are fearful when you think about money. Examples include an inability to budget, fear of checking an account balance or fear of openly talking about money. A healthy relationship with money is feelings of confidence and peace of mind. This is because money allows one the freedom to do what they want, when they want with whom they want.

Ask yourself or write out - "*What are my thoughts, feelings, and attitudes towards money?*"

A TIP FOR QUICKLY ESTABLISHING A POSITIVE RELATIONSHIP WITH MONEY

Whenever you first receive money, either from a bank or paycheck, hold it up to your nose, smell it and repeat for 17 seconds the affirmation -

"*I am one with a tremendous amount of money.*"

This simple little affirmation has worked for thousands of people wanting more money quickly.

RECEIVING MONEY AT THE POINT OF EXHANGE
CARRY LARGE NOTES

Carry in your wallet $100 to $300 in large bills and go to the mall and visit stores of items that interest you. When you see the item say to yourself "*I can afford that*" or "*I can afford the down-payment on that*". Once again you need not buy the items, but instead just pretend that you are able to.

If you drive by an expensive house or see a luxury automobile, instead of saying - "*I'll never be able to afford that!!*". Instead imagine yourself living into the millionaire dollar version of yourself. Other examples include -

"I choose not to buy this at this time"

or

"I align myself with the millionaire version of me"

"I can afford this, even if I don't know how at the moment"

If you walk by a 5 star luxury hotel or resort -

"I am pleased this hotel exists. I am thrilled for the people checking into it at this very moment!"

THE 80/20 RULE

When things are going good and you want the momentum to continue, you may find some things start to lose their effectiveness after a while or better techniques come along that enhance productivity.

If you find yourself with an overwhelming schedule, trying to keep up, get rid of what is slowing you down, and keep what is working the best. Recognize the 20% of actions you are taking which are yielding the best results, and get rid of the other 80% of actions that may be slowing you down or hindering your progress. This is known as the 80/20 rule and is a great way to maintain healthy productivity. The other antidote to this is to only stick to the

People forget what you routinely say or do; however, people will always remember who made them feel good.

priorities and the little things will eventually work themselves out.

The opposite is also true. 20% of what you keep stored away and don't use is called upon at some time in the future to fulfill a task that will eventually yield 80% in productivity. For example a snow plough is kept in storage about 10 months out of every year.

RESISTING THE URGE TO SPEND MONEY

From personal experience, I have found that besides drafting up a monthly budget, reciting the **Abundance Prayer** eliminates urges to unnecessarily spend money. The Abundance Prayer video on YouTube has more than 1 million views, so the prayer appears to work extremely well. The abundance prayer can also be said to eliminate uncertainty about the future or if one experiences any anxiety regarding money or their earning ability.

The reason the Abundance Prayer works is because as it is recited the mind enters a state of prosperity consciousness. The key is that as the words are spoken, they create a new financial blueprint that you end up moving towards. This is why it is key to choose your words carefully when you are in a state of abundance consciousness. Another prayer that is popular is the: **Prayer for a Financial Miracle**. Both these prayers can be found online   in   video   format.

AIMING FOR 100% PERFECTION IS THE ENEMY OF PROFITABILITY

While this may sound counter-intuitive, it has proven very true in the manufacturing of new inventions and products. For example the first I-phones or the first generation of Microsoft Software had numerous bugs and technical issues. By the time versions 3 and 4 were released, many (but not all) of the technical glitches and bugs had been worked out. By 2017 Windows Software almost never crashed. The same was with the automobile, the electric car and so on….. After something has been invented, and the prototype functions reasonably well, and that it is deemed safe and satisfactory, it should be released to a limited number of people. During this time feedback from customers generates the motivation necessary to develop a better next generation product.

GALES DIRECTORY OF BROADCAST MEDIA

If you are a marketing type business, the **Gales Directory of Broadcast Media** is a goldmine of statistics. This directory identifies print and broadcast sources of news and advertising for trade, labor and businesses. It includes each state of the United States sorted by **income, age, zip code** and much more.

INVESTING IN DIVIDENDS

If you have money to invest, some people will invest in dividend payouts. For example, the **S&P Global** has paid a dividend each year since the year 1937. It is one of fewer than 24 companies in the S&P 500 that increased its dividend each year for at least the last 47 years. There is also a new dividend called **Dividend Aristocrats** and **ETF (NOBL)** which focuses on companies in the S&P 500 that have raised their dividends for a minimum of 25 consecutive years. Dividend payouts allow you to get a monthly, yearly or half yearly payout of a companies' stock, usually in check form. Although it is out of the scope of this book, I encourage you to seek out further advice from a professional when seeking to receive payouts via dividends.

GLOSSARY

PROFESSIONAL OVERCOMPENSATION.

When a person exhibits an exaggerated sense of self to cover up his or her insecurity.

THE DEFINITION OF TRUE LASTING WEALTH

Real long term lasting financial wealth is when you can consistently maintain an abundance mindset which allows you to live the good life. Over time you accumulate valuable assets which you learn to live off of and your lifestyle begins to reflect the state of who you truly are.

DEFINITION OF PROSPERITY

Having success, enjoying financial freedom and having peace of mind from future financial disaster; being well-off, well to do.

PROSPERTITY CONSCIOUSNESS?

Prosperity Consciousness is living free of the mindset of scarcity. Prosperity consciousness cannot be seen or felt only experienced with our feelings and our PERCEPTION.

ENTHUSIASM
Definition of Enthusiasm - Acting out the God Within

When enthusiasm is combined with desire or purpose, it makes one feel like anything is possible. If at first you don't feel enthusiastic, than **ACT ENTHUSIASTIC** and you will soon discover that your enthusiasm becomes contagious.

WHAT IS THE ULTIMATE AUTHORITY?

Truth and wisdom are the ultimate authority because they do not seek control or power or another. They exist free of ego and do not conflict with each other.

CONFRONTATION

Can be defined as a winning attitude, as long as one does not fear   or   seek   it.

DEFINITION OF SUCCESS

Success is never a result of entirely making money, it is primarily how successful you become at something. Hence, it could be any person who deliberately intends to do something to the very best of their ability because they made the choice to do so.

DEFINITION OF GOALS

A goal is an intended action to addresses one's needs in order to reap its benefits. Goals need clarity in order to manifest rapidly and intention to see them through. Goals coming from the right state of mind create confidence. For example, some people are motivated by unexpected circumstances, which is why these goals may manifest much faster during a crisis. Although it is much more fun to manifest though inspiration and being enthusiastic about something!!

DEFINITION OF COLLECTIVE CONSCIOUSNESS

A belief, thought or attitude that can spread to and from other people's minds; much like the contagious behavior of collective fear. Just as your new beliefs must outweigh your old beliefs, your new abundance mindset must outweigh society's collective trance if you want to take on something nobody has ever tried before.

DEFINITION OF MEMETIC BELIEFS

Memetic beliefs result in a type of cultural hypnosis. Cultural hypnosis can be either positive or negative. One example is when the culture is happy and joyful such as on New Year's Eve. The other being a worldwide pandemic.

THE BRAIN'S PREFRONTAL CORTEX

The brain's left pre-frontal cortex is the part that lights up when we seek to find a solution to a problem. Humans are the only mammal on the planet that can fully access this part of the brain and use it. On the other hand, the one trait that we do share with animals is that mammals have an Amygdala.

Learning about your Brain's Frontal Lobe

The Frontal Lobe of our brain is the 40% of our entire brain. It is the creative center and lights up when we demonstrate our free will. On a day-to-day basis, the unconscious software programming we receive early on in our childhood is operating at about 90% of the time, with our frontal lobe operating about 10% of the time.

Learning to Activate your Brain's Frontal Lobe

Speculating possibilities or asking questions activates the brain's Frontal Lobe. As it does so, it begins drawing on past experiences and memories and puts these pieces together to create a new form of consciousness, which in turn drives intention.

Did you know? Dogs do not have big frontal lobes.

Research by Professor Matthew Rushworth of Oxford University's Department of Experimental Psychology discovered that the auditory parts of the brain show a strong connection with the human prefrontal cortex, but much to a lesser extent in the macaque (a monkey). Perhaps this is why listening to music helps enhance creativity and find practical solutions.

Reference

Happy creativity: Listening to happy music facilitates divergent thinking. Simone M. Ritter and Sam Ferguson. September 2017.

One's willingness to strive to be their best creates a better life for the world overall. Thank you for participating in this grand experiment of life and making the world a better place. I sincerely wish you the very BEST in any personal financial endeavor you undertake, including any personal challenge you seek to overcome!!

Scott Rauvers

Author

Notes